Boulevard
PHOTOGRAPHIC

Jim Williams

Motorbooks International
Publishers & Wholesalers

First published in 1997 by Motorbooks International Publishers & Wholesalers, 729 Prospect Avenue, PO Box 1, Osceola, WI 54020-0001 USA

Library of Congress Cataloging-in-Publication Data

Williams, Jim.
     Boulevard Photographic : the art of automotive advertising / Jim Williams
       p. cm.
     Includes Index.
     ISBN 0-7603-0305-3 (alk. paper)
     1. Advertising photography--United States--History--20th century.
2. Boulevard Photographic (Firm) 3. McGuire, Mickey. 4. Northmore, Jimmy. 5. Advertising--Automobiles--United States-- History--20th century. 6. Photography of automobiles--History--20th century. I. Title.
TR690.4.W55 1997
778.9'9629222'0922--dc21   97-16672

On the front cover: Despite all appearances, this Mickey McGuire shot of a Chrysler 300 was made under the midday sun. A combination of indoor-type flash and film lends the illusion of dusk.

On the frontispiece: Mickey McGuire shot of the 1965 Mustang.

On the title page: Jim Northmore and Art Director Mack Stanley brought these painters and this Cutlass together as part of an Oldsmobile campaign.

On the back cover: The incredibly large and complex set for this 1958 Lincoln shoot was constructed in the Eastern Michigan University fieldhouse. Several sets were used, each requiring a week to construct.

Edited by Zack Miller
Designed by Katie Finney

Printed in Hong Kong through World Print, Ltd.

CONTENTS

ACKNOWLEDGMENTS

Regardless of what's being sold, the objectives of advertising are invariably the same. The idea is to induce a consumer to take some sort of action by attracting attention, arousing interest, and creating desire.

Given that everyone is after the same thing, it's easy to see why those with something to sell have always been so eager to exploit any new communications device or medium. Therefore, the work of Jimmy Northmore, Mickey McGuire, and their company— Boulevard Photographic—could be considered significant solely on the basis that it provided the keys that unlocked so many of the technical riddles that kept photography and automobile advertising apart for more than a half-century.

Northmore and McGuire, however, did more than just bring cars and cameras together. They transformed the perception and reality of photography from that of a means of recording images, to a medium for creating virtually anything that could be imagined. In the process they not only advanced the art of automotive advertising, they expanded our automotive dreams and visions.

The pictures in most books serve to illustrate a story. However, in *Boulevard Photographic: The Art of Automobile Advertising,* the pictures are the story. So this book is dedicated to Mickey McGuire and Jimmy Northmore—two men whose determination and prowess changed the way we look at automobiles and photography. My thanks to them for their cooperation and for making the pictures that make this book.

I wish to express my gratitude to Paula Dyba for all her assistance in managing and merging what started out as a massive pile of pictures and a mere jumble of words. Thanks are also due Wally Sternicki, Jack Weber, and Louise Hirsch for helping piece together the parts and people in the story of Boulevard Photographic; Henry Obidzinski of Color Detroit for his photographic and reproduction services; and Mark Patrick, curator of the National Automotive History Collection at the Detroit Public Library, for his archival help. Finally, I'd like to thank everyone at Motorbooks International who played a part in getting the art and magic of Boulevard Photographic onto the pages which follow.

—*Jim Williams*

FOREWORD

MICKEY McGUIRE (left) AND JIMMY NORTHMORE ON A SHOOT IN CALIFORNIA, circa 1980.

Fifty years ago I was mopping the floors and mixing the chemicals in a photographic studio. If anyone had told me then that my work might one day be the subject of a book, I would have laughed. But here I am, 50 years later, writing the foreword to a book that's about my work, that of my partner, Jimmy Northmore, and our company, Boulevard Photographic.

Jimmy and I are two completely different types of people. When we first met, about the only thing we had in common was that we both somehow managed to end up in the photographic business. But as we grew into photographers, and became owners and partners in a fledgling automotive photo studio, our differences seemed to balance each other perfectly. I was the businessman, and he was the facilities man. I had a total of two assistants my entire career; Jimmy had many, most of whom he trained to become photographers in our company and sent out to the field in search of fame and fortune. Jimmy was also the inventor and mechanical wizard, solving some of the early challenges we faced in proving ourselves and photography to clients. I was and still am the spokesman, representing the studio at any given event or activity. We always worked really well together and have been partners for nearly 45 years. There again, if anyone told me this was possible, I wouldn't have believed them. Particularly in a business characterized by ups and downs—too much or too little money, too much or too little work.

In the course of our careers, we traveled through a business that was virtually nonexistent when we started, and on the verge of disappearing when we stopped. By this I mean that when we set up shop in the early 1950s, photographs were a rarity in car ads. Illustrations were the visuals of choice, because artists could do things such as make a car appear to be 35 feet long—things that no one had thought possible with photography. So we made it our job to develop the techniques necessary to demonstrate the viability of photography. And to sell as much of it as we could to advertising art directors and car companies.

We were fortunate to have started out at a time when there were art directors like John MacClure and Odie James on Nash, Mack Stanley on Packard, and Fred Peck on Dodge, who were willing to give us and photography a chance. Later, we were privileged to have clients like Andy Nelson of J. Walter Thompson, Ford's advertising agency, who wanted us to push the photographic envelope. He gave us the flexibility to be interpretive and artistic with the medium. Today, however, the challenges of creating the perfect image on film are becoming no longer relevant. In much the same evolutionary way that photography replaced the use of illustrations in advertising, the production of original photographic art is diminishing daily at the hands of computer technology. A multiplicity of techniques and computer-generated or retouched elements are now the basis for creativity. And while I can appreciate and even marvel at the results, I'd have to say that as automobile advertising photographers, our careers were perfectly timed—in at the beginning, out at the end.

Today, Jimmy and I are both officially retired from the photography business. He divides his time between Michigan and Florida, building and flying radio-controlled airplanes. I live in the paradise of Palm Springs, California, where I can play tennis every day.

Photography has never been, nor will it ever be, a hobby for either of us. So this book qualifies as a sort of love of labor. It was hard work. I can honestly say that freezing in the pre-dawn to set up for a photo shoot, or boiling on the dry lake beds of the desert was nothing compared to the past year of working on this project. I'd like to thank Walter Sternicki, my long-time assistant and loyal Boulevard employee, for all his help in sorting things out and getting things together. Of course I would also like to thank the author, Jim Williams, and Motorbooks International for giving us one last big exposure. We hope you enjoy it!

Here's to 50 years at f/16.

—*Mickey McGuire, Palm Springs, California*

INTRODUCTION
SEEING IS BELIEVING

THE POWER OF ASSOCIATION
If you don't like stripes you might not give Dodge's Viper GTS a second look.

Objectively, we know that any automobile is just an assemblage of parts. What really defines a car or truck is how its various bits are actually designed and arranged. Yet we also know that what we think and how we might feel about a particular vehicle—as with virtually anything else—isn't purely objective.

For example, you come upon a picture of a car that you've never seen before. You're looking at a two-dimensional image, so you obviously can't thump on the fenders, sit in the driver's seat, or stand on the gas. What you can see, however, is that this car has a pair of broad stripes running up its hood and over the roof. You've seen such stripes before on high-performance vehicles, and this makes a positive association in your mind. Given this, there's a good chance that your initial reaction to this otherwise unknown vehicle will be favorable, or it may, at least, warrant a second look. On the other hand, if you consider performance an irrelevant transportation trait, you may just turn the page and never give this car a second thought.

Of course, what we respond to isn't always as obvious as a pair of big stripes. We can be drawn to or repelled by any number of more subtle things—like a vehicle's proportions, its color, or the environment in which it's pictured. We're likely to think differently if a car is shown in the pits at a race track instead of in front of a posh hotel. We can also be influenced by what we read or is said about a vehicle, its name—a Cobra versus a Town Car—or our previous knowledge or experience with the make or model.

It's no mystery that this is how our minds work. The ability to remember and the inclination to associate one thing with another is what allows us to learn things. And based on what we know or think we know, we formulate opinions and make choices. That's why it's not surprising that so much of the human experience has had to do with the give and take of information.

Early on, primitive man figured out that communication via grunts and gestures could be augmented or clarified with illustrations. The problem was, and continues to be, that illustrating things via drawing or painting takes more time and ability than everyone possesses. So, as time went on, oral and written languages evolved and emerged. This allowed the graphically-challenged to use words and numbers to describe and identify things, which expanded and greatly facilitated communications. Still, most of us (with the possible exception of writers and mathematicians) tend to instinctively side with Confucius—believing that a picture is worth a thousand words.

Of course, not all pictures are equally worthy in terms of their communication value or credibility. We may believe our own eyes, but we tend to have less confidence in the vision of others. We can admire the deftness of an artist, but an image rendered by the hand of another is not the same as seeing the real thing. Thus, it's little wonder that having the means to *take* pictures directly from reality should have been one of man's oldest desires. In fact, the roots of what we call photography, which literally means "writing with light," go back as far as the dream of auto-mobility.

It's known, for example, that Leonardo da Vinci concerned himself with both cameras and mechanized conveyances. Despite da Vinci's example, those who would pursue the invention of photography and the automobile would rarely be one and the same. The development of the two technologies would, however, proceed apace until they would ultimately emerge as products of the technical and industrial revolutions of the nineteenth century. In fact, the patents for the first practical automobile (Carl Benz's *Motorwagen*) and George Eastman's first "Kodak" camera occurred within just two years of one another: in 1886 and 1888, respectively.

That photography and the automobile should have "arrived" together seemingly should have been like *kismet*. After all, the obstacles faced by the first automobile makers weren't limited to making and perfecting these new-fangled devices. The selling of the automobile, much less a particular make or model, represented a major communications challenge.

Automobiles may have been the answer to an age-old dream, but this didn't spell instant or automatic acceptance. Word that there suddenly were things that could put old dobbins out to pasture, revolutionize transportation, and re-order life itself was initially greeted with a fair degree of skepticism and even disdain. Adding to the public's auto-wariness was the competition that sprung up between pioneer auto makers, many of whom advanced conflicting notions of what an automobile ought to be. Should the ideal car have three, four, or more wheels? A tiller or a steering wheel? Internal combustion, steam, or electric power? And compounding the difficulty was the fact that the first car makers were trying to sell things the likes of which people had never seen before.

Since seeing goes such a long way toward believing, it's indeed hard to imagine that photography wouldn't always have been the focal point and mainstay of automotive advertising. However, after an initial flirtation, photography and automobile advertising would remain virtual strangers for a very long time. In fact, it would take more than a half-century before the automobile industry and the public would finally begin to see what they had been missing. And when they did, it was thanks largely to the art and magic of two men—Mickey McGuire and Jimmy Northmore—and their company—Boulevard Photographic.

1 BEFORE BOULEVARD

REGARDLESS of how many words a picture may actually be worth, its value as a means of communication is ultimately limited by the number of people who see it.

The birth of what the world would come to know as photography is usually associated with the invention of the daguerreotype. In 1839, Monsieur Louis Jacques Mandé Daguerre presented his method for capturing and fixing images on silvered copper plates to the French Academy of Sciences. The French government bought Daguerre's invention and offered it to the world (except to England) free of charge. The process was slow and cumbersome, but no one doubted that daguerreotypes reflected reality.

The invention of the daguerreotype made it possible to record images without drawing them, but those images would have been little more than wall decorations had photographic processes not also held the key to unlocking the power of the press.

More than a decade before Daguerre revealed his method for taking pictures to the world, a man who would briefly be his partner, Joseph Niepce, invented the process of *photo gravure* or photoengraving. In 1826, he found that shining light through a line drawing and onto a metal plate coated with bitumen left a latent image which, after development and etching, yielded an engraved surface that could then be inked and printed. This meant it would no longer be necessary to manually cut or engrave a surface in order to produce a printable image. Daguerre, however, was not particularly interested in printing or publishing. Artists and printers, however, were quick to see the value of Niepce's discovery. By the 1870s, photoengraving was a commercially viable process, and it had greatly expanded the use of illustrations in advertising and in newspapers, magazines, and books.

Photoengraving did not by itself mean printers were ready or able to reproduce photographs. And the reason was that then, as now, normal printing presses could imprint ink only in uniform density. This means it is impossible for a printing press to literally reproduce shadings. Such can only be simulated by imprinting ink in varying patterns. For centuries, artists and engravers had used solid lines of different widths and lengths to give the illusion of shadings. Photoengraving could easily reproduce such "line" art, but the reproduction of illustrations comprised of tones hinged upon another development—the screen or halftone conversion process.

The halftone process involves the use of a mask or screen to break up or convert continuous tones of varying darkness (as in a photograph) into a continuous pattern of constant density but varying area. Thus, what the eye sees as lighter or darker tones are actually produced by smaller or larger dots that are uniformly spaced, but occupy a lesser or greater amount of a given area.

The first person known to have made a halftone photoengraving was an Englishman, Fox Talbot. He is also credited with inventing the negative-positive process that the world would eventually come to accept as photography. Unlike Daguerre's process, in which the camera captured a positive image on a metal plate, Talbot's recorded a negative image in the camera from which positive prints could be made. Talbot revealed his process in the same year Daguerre introduced his. However, due in part to Talbot's compulsion to patent and guard the use of his ideas, Daguerre's process was more enthusiastically embraced.

Talbot nevertheless persisted and, in an effort to gain recognition, decided to publish examples of his work. In order to do so, it was necessary for him to devise a means by which his photographic images could be reproduced on a printing press. In the process, he discovered that photographic tones could be converted into a printable "dot pattern" by laying a screen of fine gauze material over a light-sensitive engraving plate before exposing it to one of his paper negatives. In 1844 he used this method—which he called "photoglyphy"—to produce a number of halftone engravings for *The Pencil of Nature*, the first book ever to be illustrated with printed photos. He continued to refine his process and, true to form, patented it. This, combined with the lack of acceptance of his positive-negative photographic process, served to deter the development and application of halftone engraving for more than two decades. In fact, it wasn't until the 1870s that another halftone photoengraving was published. In December 1873, *The Daily Graphic*, New York City's first "picture" newspaper, used a lined glass screen to photoengrave and print a simple black-and-white photo.

In the context of other inventions, the halftone screen may seem like a minor discovery. However, in terms of spreading awareness, knowledge, and understanding, its significance ranks with the invention of the printing press and movable type.

Thanks to the halftone process, virtually anything that could be photographed—including the work of artists and illustrators—could now be directly reproduced and published. And even though photography itself would remain primarily a black-and-white medium for the better part of a half-century, it was not long before it was found that the screen or halftone principle could be applied to print things in color. In fact, before Henry Ford built his first car, process four-color printing was already a reality. The basic idea behind halftone engravings and color separations would also be the starting point for future technologies that would ultimately allow images to appear on television and computer screens. However, the immediate and significant impact of the halftone was that it ushered in the era of "photojournalism."

Suddenly, images were not just the companion of words, they were at least their rival and often their better. Pictures reached out in ways that words couldn't. People who had previously lacked the time, inclination, or the ability to read such things as newspapers and magazines were suddenly looking at them and buying them in droves. The birth of photojournalism generated a tremendous increase in both the variety and circulation of publications. This, in turn, led to a boom for the advertising industry. The age of invention and mass production was changing the world and people wanted to see what was going on and what new things were for sale.

Initially, photographs were a common sight in automobile ads. Needing to convince the public that automobiles and the companies that made them were real, early car ads routinely offered up simple photographs as if to say that "a particular maker had actually made a car." But as people accepted the reality of automobiles and as competition between makes

PHOTOGRAPHY WASN'T ALWAYS THE ANSWER
The victim of slow film speeds and crude cameras, many people assumed this 1904 Cadillac was stuck on the steps of the nation's Capitol. *National Automotive History Collection, Detroit Public Library*

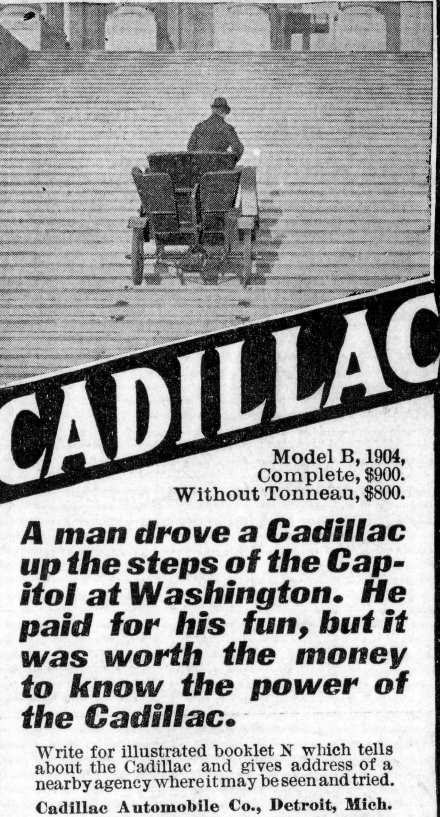

CADILLAC

Model B, 1904,
Complete, $900.
Without Tonneau, $800.

A man drove a Cadillac up the steps of the Capitol at Washington. He paid for his fun, but it was worth the money to know the power of the Cadillac.

Write for illustrated booklet N which tells about the Cadillac and gives address of a nearby agency where it may be seen and tried.

Cadillac Automobile Co., Detroit, Mich.
Member Association of Licensed Automobile Manufrs.

developed, ads were called upon to do much more. And when they were, it was discovered that the powers of photography could sometimes be difficult to harness.

In 1904, Henry M. Leland's Cadillac Automobile Company was barely two years old, but it was already feeling the pressure of competition. The problem was multi-cylinder engines were suddenly the rage, but Cadillac still offered only a "single." At the time there were no regulations on fair, or even polite, advertising practices, and Cadillac had come under fire from the competition. Cadillac's agency decided to fight back. After a couple tries, it came up with an ad that admonished people to not believe claims that "a Cadillac lacks power" or that "the company was about to remodel its engine." The ad appeared in different sizes. In the largest version, a copywriter explained how even the previous year's engine was capable of extraordinary feats of power and cited the example of a man in Canton, Ohio, who easily pulled 8 tons of railway steel with his single-cylinder Cadillac while a competitor's twin-cylinder model failed to move the same load so much as an inch. The most widely seen versions dispensed with such copy, and merely featured a photograph and a boldface caption which read: "A man drove a Cadillac up the steps of the Capitol at Washington. He paid for his fun, but it was worth the money to know the power of the Cadillac."

Records show that Cadillac sales in 1904 were some 500 more than in 1903. So it would be hard to say that this ad ruined Cadillac's fortunes, but contemporary reports indicate that it didn't have the desired effect. Although it is impossible to know for sure why this photo was used, it's reasonable to assume that the ad agency

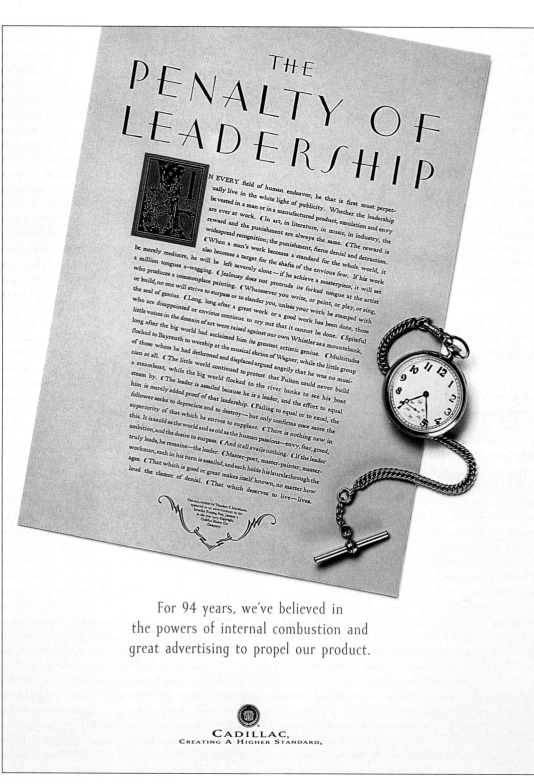

SETTING THE STANDARD FOR THE WORLD

Rather than using photography to address a marketing problem, John F. MacManus wrote a Cadillac ad in 1915 that didn't even mention a car, much less show one. "The Penalty of Leadership" would become an enduring element in Cadillac's advertising efforts, as evidenced by its appearance in this ad from 1996. *Cadillac Motor Division*

Somewhere West of Laramie

SOMEWHERE west of Laramie there's a broncho-busting, steer-roping girl who knows what I'm talking about.

She can tell what a sassy pony, that's a cross between greased lightning and the place where it hits, can do with eleven hundred pounds of steel and action when he's going high, wide and handsome.

The truth is—the Playboy was built for her.

Built for the lass whose face is brown with the sun when the day is done of revel and romp and race.

She loves the cross of the wild and the tame.

There's a savor of links about that car—of laughter and lilt and light—a hint of old loves—and saddle and quirt. It's a brawny thing—yet a graceful thing for the sweep o' the Avenue.

Step into the Playboy when the hour grows dull with things gone dead and stale.

Then start for the land of real living with the spirit of the lass who rides, lean and rangy, into the red horizon of a Wyoming twilight.

JORDAN

JORDAN MOTOR CAR COMPANY, *Inc.*, *Cleveland*, *Ohio*

thought it would lend veracity to Cadillac's claims. Unfortunately, it had just the opposite effect. People believed what they saw in photographs and, due to the slowness of the films and the rudimentary cameras that were available at the time, what people saw was a car that appeared to be parked on the Capitol steps. As a result, the photo was widely regarded as a sham. The reaction might have been different had the same picture appeared in a news report of how a Cadillac had actually been driven up the Capitol steps by a young man who had been plied with cash and hard cider by an enterprising adman, and that man was arrested and fined by the D.C. police. But in the context of an advertisement, the photo was anything but convincing evidence of Cadillac speed and power.

Cadillac's 1904 ad may have been ill-conceived, but the fact that the photo seems to have been the one and only thing that made it notable should have been a ringing endorsement for the use of photography in advertising. Of course, in hindsight it's easy to see that the problem was that the photo was poorly executed. At the time, however, there were plenty of people in the advertising business who were relieved and eager to say that photography had no place in advertising.

Thus, it was not too surprising that more than a decade after the Capitol steps debacle—when an ad was once again called for to defend the Cadillac name—photography would not be part of the picture.

In 1909 Cadillac became part of William Durant's General Motors organization. With Buick and Oldsmobile already in the GM fold, Cadillac was earmarked to become the top brand. In keeping with this strategy, Cadillac debuted a number of advancements, including Delco electrics, the self-starter, and finally in 1914, a V-8 engine. Although Cadillac couldn't lay claim to offering the world's first V-8, its high-speed design was still the kind of thing that wowed the public and stood to elevate the marque's stature. Unfortunately, Cadillac's V-8 initially suffered reliability problems—including self-immolation—which some competitors, most notably Packard, were quick to point out and try to exploit.

The ad created to address this situation didn't even mention a car, much less show one. Written by Theodore F. MacManus, the ad was entitled, "The Penalty of Leadership," and it merely spoke about the reward and punishments of being a leader. The reward was recognition; the punishments were denial, detraction, and the envy of lesser competitors. Cadillac was deluged with requests for reprints. "The Penalty of Leadership" went on to became a staple in Cadillac's advertising efforts for a number of years, and many would ultimately credit it with cementing Cadillac's image as the "Standard of the World."

In 1945, the advertising trade journal *Printer's Ink* celebrated its 50th anniversary, and on that occasion it asked readers to name the greatest advertisement of all time. Three ads finished in a virtual dead heat. First was "The Penalty of Leadership." Next was an ad written by Raymond Rubicam that launched the E. R. Squibb company into the over-the-counter medicine business. And third was another automotive ad, Edward S. "Ned" Jordan's famous "Somewhere West of Laramie" ad.

Ned Jordan presided over the Jordan Motor Car Company of Cleveland, Ohio, and that firm's advertising, from its founding in 1916 until it would become a casualty of the depression in 1931. He created many ads, but this, his most famous, first appeared in the June 23, 1923, issue of the *Saturday Evening Post*. As such, it came in the midst of a good, but not great, year for his company. According to the somewhat sketchy data available, 6,691 Jordans were sold during 1923, which was about 2,000 more than those sold in 1922, but only a little more than half the number sold in the company's best year—1926. In its entire existence, Jordan sold only about 50,000 vehicles. By comparison, the Ford Motor Company's sales topped 1.1 million in 1923 alone. So, in objective terms, one can say that Jordan was never hugely successful. Thus, one may well wonder why, to this day, this ad would be considered one of the greatest of all time and finds its way into virtually every discussion of automotive advertising.

It's usually said that "Somewhere West of Laramie" deserves its place in history because Jordan relied on "emotion" instead of "nuts and bolts" to sell a car. And while he certainly did that, MacManus and others had done so long before. The fact is, advertising people came to revere "Somewhere West of Laramie" because the public loved the ad far more than they did the car it advertised. And the thing they loved most were Jordan's words.

SERIOUS TIMES CALLED FOR SERIOUS ADS

In 1932, five decades before Chrysler President Lee Iacocca assumed the role of TV pitch man, Walter P. Chrysler appeared as an earnest corporate spokesman for Plymouth. The ads, created by the agency started by J. Stirling Getchell, are credited with establishing Plymouth as a serious competitor to Chevrolet and Ford. Getchell, however, would not live to see the age of TV advertising. He, like Chrylser, succumbed to ill-health just before the onset of World War II. *National Automotive History Collection, Detroit Public Library*

"Any car that hasn't Patented Floating Power is Out-of-Date"

—Walter P. Chrysler

WALTER P. CHRYSLER BACKS HIS BELIEF BY ASKING YOU TO DRIVE ALL THREE LOWEST-PRICED CARS AND LEARN HOW VIBRATION IS CONQUERED IN ONE—THE PLYMOUTH

WHEN I STATE my conviction that *any* car that hasn't patented Floating Power is *out-of-date*, I deliberately challenge every competitor of the New 1932 Plymouth.

There is only one genuine Floating Power. That is the revolutionary engine mounting created by Chrysler Motors engineers *exclusively* for Plymouth, De Soto, Dodge and Chrysler cars.

Plymouth's Floating Power is an advantage found in *no other* car in Plymouth's price class.

Floating Power makes Plymouth the *one* lowest-priced car free of body vibration. It gives the New Plymouth the smoothness of a high-priced eight.

Prove this for yourself. Drive a Plymouth with Floating Power. Note its utter lack of vibration. Then drive any other with old-fashioned engine mountings—and see the difference.

Besides Floating Power, the New Plymouth includes every feature that the most modern car can have.

Its 112-inch wheelbase accommodates a larger and roomier Safety-Steel body. Plymouth is a *big* car. It's a beautiful car—far smarter than any car in its price class.

The New Plymouth has increased power—greater speed, faster get-away, greater all-around performance.

I want you to *drive* the New 1932 Plymouth. I think it's the easiest-riding automobile I have ever driven. I'd like *your* opinion, too.

And I'm also sure you'll be enthusiastic about its easy handling. With Free Wheeling, the new Automatic Clutch, the Silent-Second, Easy-Shift Transmission, Plymouth is a real joy to drive. And Hydraulic Brakes make you so much safer and surer.

I urge you to go and *see* this car. Compare it with the other two cars in the lowest-priced field. Drive it. See for yourself why your Plymouth dollar buys more.

With Patented FLOATING POWER . . . 65-H. P. Engine Free Wheeling . . . Silent-Second, Easy-Shift Transmission Safety-Steel Bodies . . . Rigid-X Double-Drop Frame Hydraulic Brakes with Centrifuse Brake Drums . . . 112-inch Wheelbase . . . Optional Equipment at Slight Extra Cost: Automatic Clutch $8; Duplate Safety Plate Glass, Coupe $9.50, 4-door Sedan $17.50.

10 MODELS — Business Roadster $495, Business Coupe $565, 2-door Sedan $575, Sport Roadster $595, Sport Phaeton $595, Coupe (with rumble seat) $610, 4-door Sedan $635, Convertible Coupe $645, 7-passenger Sedan (121-inch wheelbase) $725, Convertible Sedan $785. THRIFT MODELS — 2-door Sedan $495, 4-door Sedan $575. All prices f. o. b. factory. Low delivered prices. Convenient time-payments. All enclosed models wired for Philco-Transitone radio without extra cost.

OF COURSE, you're listening to Chrysler Motors Radio Program "Ziegfeld Radio Show," personally conducted by Flo Ziegfeld — Columbia Coast-to-Coast Network — every Sunday evening.

Plymouth's Chief Engineer congratulates the Operating Manager for the excellence of workmanship maintained in the manufacture of Plymouth cars.

4-DOOR SEDAN, $635

PLYMOUTH $495

AND UP, F. O. B. FACTORY — SOLD BY DESOTO · DODGE · CHRYSLER DEALERS

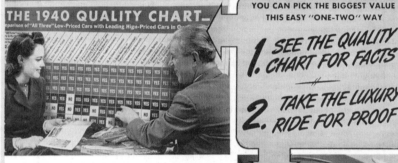

USING PHOTOGRAPHS TO TELL A STORY

The prewar ads produced by Getchell and his agency were invariably built around photographs that weren't used merely to show a product. In this 1940 ad, the car shares equal billing with Plymouth's "quality chart" and a satisfied Plymouth customer. Getchell believed that people wanted realism, which was best shown by "simple photographs that the eye can read and the mind can understand."

"Somewhere West of Laramie" served to confirm that clever copy was key to advertising success. The positive response to Jordan's romantic style inspired scores of imitators until the Depression introduced the harsh tone of reality.

In 1931, the same year in which Ned Jordan closed his company, a new advertising agency was opened by another visionary named J. Stirling Getchell. Although Getchell's specialty was copy, he wasn't wedded to the flowery style advanced by the followers of Jordan in the 1920s, nor did he question the value of art directors. Thus, Getchell opened his new agency with himself and an art director named Jack Tarleton as partners. In 1932, Getchell and Tarleton took on a third partner, Orrin Kilbourn, who brought in business from Chrysler's DeSoto division. Thanks to Kilbourn's connections, that same year they were given a one-shot assignment to introduce that year's new Plymouth. Launched in 1928, Plymouth was intended to be Chrysler's volume leader, but so far it had not been taken seriously by Ford and Chevy buyers. Getchell's charge was to change this perception.

Though Getchell came up with many concepts and headlines, it is Tarleton who is credited with coming up with the idea that would ultimately put Plymouth on the map. The headline merely said, "Look at all three!" and it appeared above a starkly lit photo of Walter P. Chrysler leaning over the hood of a new Plymouth. The copy, written by Getchell, quoted Chrylser with technical reasons why anyone should prefer a Plymouth over its unnamed competition. The ad first appeared in April 1932, and by June, Plymouth sales were 218 percent better than the year before. He and Tarleton were assigned another ad. They again featured a photograph of Walter P. Chrysler, but this time with the claim that "Any car that hasn't Patented Floating Power is Out-of-Date." Plymouth sales rose again, and as a result Getchell and Tarleton were awarded the entire Plymouth account. Later, Getchell would pen the line, "Plymouth sets the pace for all three," which gave further rise to Plymouth's fortune while originating the concept of the "Big Three."

In making ads, Getchell always started with photographs—dozens, even hundreds of them. Eventually, the agency would build up an enormous cross-index file of all kinds of photos. Typefaces and headlines would be built around the pictures, followed last by the copy. He also believed in hiring the best photographers, including the likes of Margaret Burke White, who shot photos for DeSoto ads. Getchell liked his ads with "bounce"—ads that came off the page fast. That usually meant tabloid formats, fast and punchy copy, and above all, photographs. Getchell has been quoted as saying: "We believe people want realism today. Events portrayed as they happen. Products as they really are. Human interest. People. Places. Told in simple photographs that the eye can read and the mind can understand."

Through the 1930s Getchell's words were taken to heart by many in the automotive advertising business. But after World War II, people were inclined to see things differently. Although the war only interrupted car production for four years, America was a much different place when the car companies went back into business. Prosperity and pent-up demand left consumers eager to buy new cars. But people had different expectations and wanted more power, more style, more everything. The conservative influence of the prewar years had vanished. Unfortunately, the cars coming out of Detroit were four-year-old designs, penned at a time when conservatism and functionality ruled the day. The last thing people wanted to see, or manufacturers wanted to show, were stark photographs of cars that reflected prewar designs and Depression-era thinking. So, initially, the auto companies reverted to using illustrations in their ads to make the best of a bad situation. But even when manufacturing caught up and cars began to reflect postwar taste, there still remained the challenge of merging the art of photography and the art of automotive imagery.

The reasons why photography and automobile advertising remained strangers for so long were many. Given this, one might assume that the story of what finally brought them together would be an equally convoluted tale. And although there were many factors to making automotive imagery and photography synonymous, there were very few that weren't related to the work of two photographers— Mickey McGuire and Jimmy Northmore—and their company, Boulevard Photographic.

ADDING TO THE NEW MEASURE OF VALUE
Introduced in mid-1948, "step-down" Hudsons were longer, lower, and wider than just about anything on the road. Even so, their proportions were not immune to artistic embellishment.

2 The BUILDING of BOULEVARD

THE "UNHOLY TWO"

Mickey McGuire and Jimmy Northmore appeared to be a very odd couple, as illustrated in this caricature drawn in the early 1950s by Guy Morrison, who would go on to become a noted advertising photographer in his own right.

LETTING THE GENIE OUT OF THE BOTTLE

The viability of photography as a medium for automotive advertising took a giant step forward in 1949. That's when Jimmy Northmore managed to produce "white chrome" by shooting this Mercury inside the lighting "tent" he constructed on the stage of a Detroit music hall.

THE BUILDING OF BOULEVARD

As with most people who aren't related, the meeting of Mickey McGuire and Jimmy Northmore was a matter of chance. Although they both grew up in Detroit and could be considered contemporaries—Northmore was born in 1925, McGuire in 1929—it wasn't until 1951 that fate finally brought them together at Detroit's New Center Studio.

New Center Studio was the postwar brainchild of a clever fellow named Art Greenwald, who'd managed to bring together the most sought-after automotive advertising artists in one place. His idea wasn't to capitalize on the marquee value of individual artists; rather, it was to apply their talents collectively. New Center's forte was rendering whatever a client might want or need. If this meant using one artist for the vehicle, another for the background, and still another hand to letter a headline or logo, it was all so much the better so far as Greenwald was concerned. Of course, creating such works of art required precise planning, layouts, and reference. And for these purposes, photographs were ideal and invaluable tools.

A talented layout artist could cut apart and paste together photographs to produce a reasonable facsimile of how all the parts and pieces of an illustration should go together. This not only gave artists a road map to follow, it gave clients a chance to look at and approve things before finished artwork was begun. At the layout stage, background elements could be added or subtracted; people could be made shorter, taller, or stuck in different places; photographs of vehicles could be sliced and sectioned to enhance or alter their proportions. Photography was therefore critical to the process, if not the products, of New Center Studio. This helps explain why Greenwald was so relieved when Jimmy Northmore somehow happened to show up on the very day in 1947 when the studio's photographer suddenly announced he was quitting.

A YOUNG JIMMY NORTHMORE
In 1947, Jimmy Northmore (right) and his buddy, Dick Crandall, took a vacation trip to Mackinaw Island where a chance meeting with a couple of young ladies resulted in Northmore finding his way to New Center Studio, the precursor of Boulevard Photographic.

Northmore was a mere 22 years old when he first appeared at New Center Studio, but he could already boast a fair amount of photographic experience. The son of a prominent newspaper photographer, he'd been exposed to photography from an early age. Still, he says he hadn't always dreamed of following in his father's footsteps. "My first love was airplanes. As a kid, I had no interest whatsoever in photography—I actually resented it because it kept my father away from home so much." He would, however, change his mind when he was about 16.

In his junior year of high school, Northmore had a physics teacher who ran a youth summer camp. And that spring, the teacher was looking for someone interested in a summer job. It wasn't a particularly glamorous camp, but because it was located out of state—near exotic Cincinnati, Ohio—the job portended great adventure. As a result there was no shortage of students who wanted the job. The only catch was that the position entailed the duties of camp photographer. Aware that Northmore's father was a photographer, the teacher assumed Jimmy would know how to take pictures and, thus, offered him the position. At that point, however, Northmore had never taken a photo in his life. But because he both wanted and needed the job, he accepted the offer—hoping that his father would be willing and able to turn him into a photographer before the school year was out.

Regardless of the reason for his son's sudden interest in photography, Northmore's father was happy to oblige. He pulled out one of his trusty 4x5 Speed Graphics and showed Jimmy how to cock the shutter and focus the camera. With war brewing, film was getting hard to come by, so his father got together a dozen old-fashioned glass plates, showed Jimmy how to load them, and then sent him out to the local park. After exposing all 12 plates, they went to his

THE SCHOOL OF HARD KNOCKS

Mickey McGuire dropped out of college in 1948 and went to work as a photographer's assistant, but he says he would have done anything: "I would have gone to work for an undertaker if one would have offered me a job." In this picture, McGuire (left) and another future car photographer, Warren Winstanley, act as models in a demonstration of how photographs could be made and used for artists' reference.

STARTING WITH A "WING" AND A PRAYER

Made as a sample when the financial responsibilities of parenthood forced him to seek greener pastures, this 1952 Willys Aero-Wing was the first car picture McGuire took on his own.

NEW CENTER'S TENT STUDIO

To introduce art directors and clients to his company's new photographic studio, Art Greenwald staged a show of art and photography inside the tent lighting set.

father's darkroom where Jimmy learned how to develop negatives and make prints.

That summer, Northmore discovered he not only liked but seemed to have a knack for photography. During his senior year, he more or less became his school's "official" photographer. He also started shooting such things as weddings for extra money. When he graduated from high school, America was at war. Still enamored with airplanes, he immediately enlisted in the Army Aviation Cadet

Program but found he wasn't yet old enough to be called up for active service. While waiting to turn 18, he parlayed his new-found photographic knowledge into a temporary job in General Motors' giant photographic division. There he worked in the reproduction department, which copied and duplicated all of the corporation's engineering drawings, plans, and blueprints.

After two years, World War II was winding down and Northmore was mustered out of the service. In the meantime, his father had gotten

PROMOTING ILLUSTRATION
Art Greenwald's New Center Studio was in the business of providing illustrations. But in this promotional photo, shot by a young Northmore, it's easy to overlook the futuristic rendering by one of the studio's featured artists, Art Radobough.

PIONEER COLOR PHOTOGRAPHY
Cliff Hartwell was hired by New Center Photographic because he was already a skilled car photographer and an early master of color photography. In 1950, he shot this Hudson with Northmore as his assistant.

out of the newspaper business and moved the family to Philadelphia, where he had taken a job with the Eastman Kodak Company as a technical representative. Jimmy decided to go to Philadelphia as well. There, he worked for the Charles P. Mills & Son photo studio. After about a year in the City of Brotherly Love, he decided he preferred the more familiar surroundings of the Motor City.

Once back in Detroit, Northmore went to work for a large photofinishing concern. The job was tedious and boring, but at least he was "home" and able to go places and do things with his buddies. On a vacation trip to Mackinaw Island in the summer of 1947, he and a friend happened to meet a couple of young ladies from Detroit. In the course of conversation, Northmore allowed that he was in the photographic business. He also let it be known that he wasn't very happy with his present position. To Northmore's surprise, the girls happened to know a thing or two about photography. They said they worked for an automotive art studio in Detroit that employed a photographer to shoot pictures for layouts and artists' reference. They also said they knew something that even their boss didn't know—the studio's photographer had told them he might soon quit and return to

the military. The girls promised Northmore that if this were to happen they'd be sure to let him know.

The girls were good to their word. About a week later, one of them called to say the photographer had just gone into the studio manager's office to resign. And, if Northmore was still interested in a new job, now was the time to call for an interview. He did and, given the situation, was of course seen immediately. Needless to say, the girls worked for New Center Studio. They introduced Northmore to the studio manager who hired him on the spot. Thus, by what he calls "somewhat devious means," Northmore happened to be in the right place at the right time to begin his career as an automotive photographer.

The same year Northmore started to work at New Center Studio, Mickey McGuire was graduating from high school. At that point he too had acquired some photographic experience, but photography wasn't high on a list of things he wanted to pursue. When McGuire had turned 16, he'd gotten an after-school job working for a door-to-door baby photographer. Jokingly referred to as "kidnappers," there were many such photographers who roamed communities in the immediate postwar years hoping to cash in on the then booming birthrate. Because it was such a competitive business, most kidnappers worked on "spec." They didn't charge for taking pictures, they only made money when people ordered prints. Human nature being what it is, selling prints was relatively easy. The hard part was getting people to agree to a photo session in the first place. And this was where McGuire came in. He started out as a "caller," which involved canvassing neighborhoods to identify homes where the company's photographers would be welcome. Using a made-up spiel—he would tell a proud parent that a certain milk company was thinking of replacing the cow on its label with a picture of a baby, and that his firm's photographers had been hired to find and photograph the perfect baby—McGuire proved to be a highly effective caller. So good was he, that soon he was promoted to the potentially more lucrative position of photographer. And although he quickly mastered the tricks of the trade, he didn't see baby photography as something he wished to pursue after graduating from high school.

Unsure of exactly what he wanted to do, McGuire enrolled at a local college, but before his freshman year was out, he called his older brother in desperation and said, "Do you know anybody, anywhere who will hire me for any amount of money to do anything? I can't stand any more school."

McGuire's brother was an art director for MacManus, John & Adams (MJ&A), the same agency that some three decades earlier had been responsible for Cadillac's most famous ad, "The Penalty of Leadership." The agency had gone on to become a fixture in the roster of agencies employed by GM's various divisions. And although business was good, the elder McGuire saw no immediate openings for his sibling at MJ&A. His only suggestion was that Mickey contact a photographer he knew who had just fired his assistant. Since McGuire had some photographic experience, there was a chance that this fellow might give him a job.

It turned out that the photographer was indeed looking for a new assistant, and McGuire appeared to be a reasonable candidate. He not only had a modicum of experience, he was, more importantly, strong, immensely tall (seven feet tall to be exact), highly motivated, and willing to work for any amount of money. The photographer looked McGuire up and down and said, "You can hang around here for a week, and if you don't piss me off, I'll hire you." McGuire hung around for a week. Because he proved to be more of a help than an irritation, he got the job, which he says was actually more like servitude. "He paid me twenty-five bucks a week to start and worked my butt off for three-and-a-half years. In exchange I got what amounted to a college education in the business of photography."

McGuire's mentor and taskmaster was Cleland Clark. Like Art Greenwald, he too was in the business of supplying illustrations for automotive advertising. Clark, however, had a different perspective on photography's role in the process. Even though he was not above shooting pictures that advertising art directors and artists might use for layouts and reference, Clark's stock in trade was creating photos that were themselves finished art. He was what was commonly known as a "photo illustrator."

Clark had begun shooting cars for advertising before World War II. And when the war put paid to civilian automobile production and advertising, he went to work for Uncle Sam, who was in constant need of vast numbers of clear and concise illustrations to instruct the troops on the operation and identification of all the military vehicles and hardware that were then pouring out of Detroit factories. After the war, he worked briefly for General Motors Photographic, but soon left to set up his own studio when automobile production and advertising resumed with a vengeance.

The postwar period brought a boom in advertising. In just five years—1945 to 1950—annual ad expenditures in America would nearly double. And the lion's share of the increase was attributable to car advertising. Where packaged goods and cigarettes had traditionally been the most heavily advertised products, cars were suddenly on their way to

THE BOYS OF BOULEVARD
Early Boulevard staff. Upper Row (left to right): Bud Hassard, Duane Fouraker, Jim Carter, Wally Sternicki, Mickey McGuire, Bob Schmidt, Joe Pajakowski, and Tom Halstad. Center: Bob Traniello, Richard Voikin, Guy Morrison, Jim Gran, Jimmy Northmore, and Cliff Hartwell. Lower: Joe Outland, John Wisner, Al Gran, Dick Crandall, and Henry Obidzinski.

WESTWARD EXPANSION

As Boulevard's business grew, so did its efforts to promote its services. This poster, featuring Boulevard staff, was produced soon after opening a facility in California.

address to have if you were in the automobile or advertising business. In the beginning, Northmore had been pretty much a one-man band—shooting photos for New Center's artists and then doing most of his own developing and printing in his own darkroom at home. But after the move he found himself in charge of in-house lab and darkroom facilities, plus finding and training people to operate them. And although he continued to shoot scrap for New Center's artists, he also managed to convince Greenwald that the studio had the wherewithal to at least dabble in the field of "photo illustration." Thus, New Center Photographic began shooting finished photography for smaller industrial products, primarily for non-automotive clients such as Dow Chemical Company.

Having embarked upon the business of photo illustration, albeit on a limited basis, Greenwald one day found himself talking about the pros and cons of photography with an art buyer in New York. Somewhat to his surprise, this client was of an opinion, which was then on its way to becoming accepted that fact throughout the advertising community, as for the purposes of advertising, photographs were almost always preferable to artwork.

As advertising had become a game of ever-higher stakes, it had also become the subject of considerable study. Such studies had begun before the war, and few advertising people were willing to argue with the findings of respected researchers such as Dr. George Gallup and Dr. Daniel Starch, whose research indicated that ads that employed photographs were more often noticed and believed than those that relied on illustrations. It may have chagrined some traditionalists, but even the oldest hands would ultimately agree with the likes of David Ogilvy, who opened his New York agency in 1948 and would later say in his book *Confessions of an Advertising Man*: "It grieves me to tell you not to use drawings, because I would dearly like to help artists get commissions to illustrate advertisements. But the advertisements would not sell, the clients would go broke, and then there would be no patrons left to support the artists. If you use photographs, your clients will prosper sufficiently to buy paintings to present to public galleries."

Obviously wishing for such prosperity, the client with whom Greenwald was speaking said he would endorse the use of photography whenever practical and possible. And thanks to the then-recent introduction of color films, there seemed to be few occasions when it wasn't at least possible to use photography. So far as this client was concerned, the biggest drawback to photographs in automotive advertising was "chrome."

The problem was that chromium-plated grilles, bumpers, and trim, which were then key automotive styling and selling features, rarely looked good in photographs. Their appearance was invariably marred by unwanted or unattractive reflections. The client said, "It was too bad automobiles

number one. In fact, by 1955 the first nine of America's 10 biggest advertisers would be domestic car brands, led by Chevrolet and Ford. The sheer volume of automotive advertising boded well for everyone involved in the automotive advertising business, which of course included New Center Studio. So, while McGuire was working his butt off, Northmore was also extremely busy.

Soon after Northmore came on board, New Center Studio began to expand, moving from its original quarters in the New Center Building to more copious spaces in the nearby Fisher Building, which was then the

BIGGER AND BETTER BOULEVARD STUDIOS
McGuire and Northmore eventually left Boulevard's namesake behind (the former New Center Photographic studio on Detroit's East Grand Boulevard). In 1960, Northmore came up with the features and McGuire acted as the architect for a new studio, located on Victor in Highland Park on Detroit's north side.

couldn't be shot like a piece of silverware, jewelry, or even a toaster." He was referring to the fact that photo illustrators routinely shot small metallic objects in a "tent"—an enclosure, usually of white fabric, which eliminated extraneous reflections while producing elegant white ones.

Upon returning to Detroit, a somewhat chastened Greenwald asked Northmore if he thought there was any reason why "tent lighting" couldn't be applied to automobiles. Northmore said he couldn't see any reason why it wouldn't work. But in order to test the idea, they'd need a much larger space than New Center's existing studio in the Fisher Building. Thus, the old downtown Detroit Music Hall was rented and a chrome-laden 1949 Mercury four-door sedan was forklifted up onto the stage. Once in place, Northmore fabricated a "tent" of white muslin around and over the car. To produce the desired white highlights and reflections, lights were arranged to bounce illumination through the tent. And although Northmore considered the results "a little crude," they clearly showed that, if one was willing to think big, photography could be an appropriate medium for illustrating cars.

By his own hand, Greenwald had let the photographic genie out of the bottle. The "white chrome" experiment opened a lot of eyes and a lot of doors. It was now clear that if New Center was going to stay in the automobile advertising business, it was going to have to get into finished photography. And by 1950, New Center Studio had a new photographic

THE EUROPEANS DISCOVER BOULEVARD
Automobile advertising in Europe was characterized by straight-forward, utilitarian photographs until art directors there discovered the art and magic of Boulevard Photographic. Images, like this sample "double-exposure" made by Northmore for an English Ford client, would help make Boulevard the biggest supplier of car photography in Europe.

division, the cornerstone of which was a studio located on East Grand Boulevard. It would house the first tent lighting set specifically designed to accommodate automobiles. Greenwald also went out and secured the services of a veteran car photographer named Cliff Hartwell.

Like Cle Clark, the photographer who earlier had hired McGuire, Hartwell had begun his career before the war. He had in fact worked for Photographic Illustration, Inc., a Detroit studio that had opened in 1933 and had been responsible for much of the photography that found its way into Depression-era automobile advertising. He too had gone on to further hone his skills shooting military equipment for the government during the war and had done a tour of duty at General Motors Photographic. What's more, Hartwell was also among the few photographers anywhere who had historical as well as practical experience in the processes involved in reproducing color images photographically.

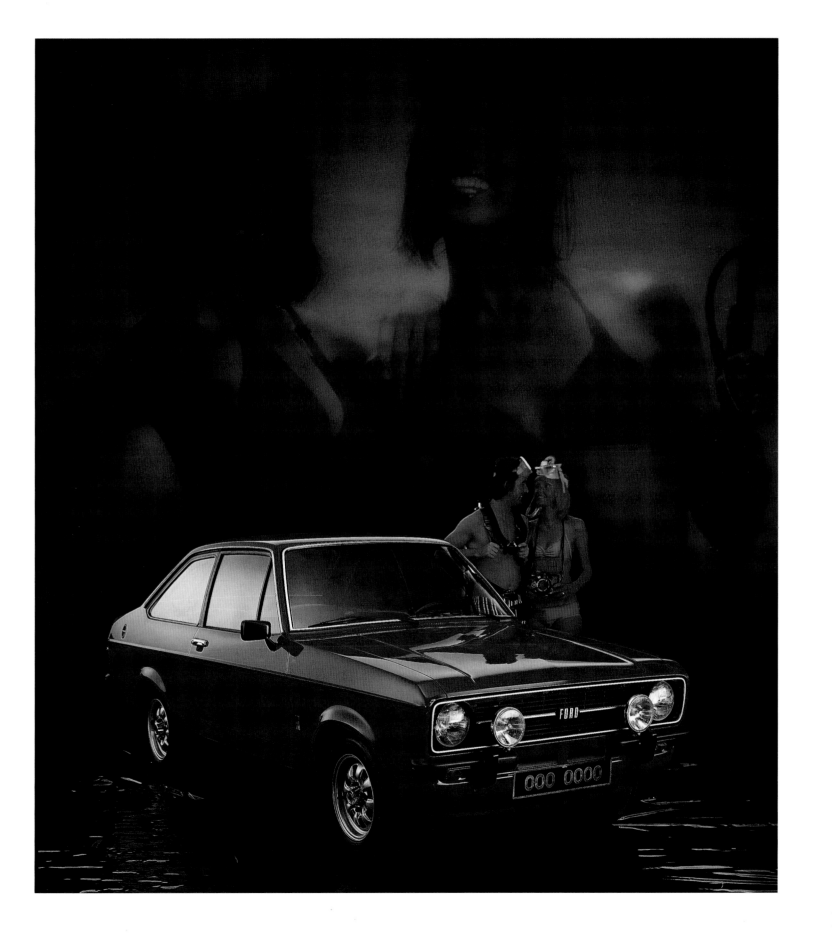

BOULEVARD
THE GANG THAT CAN SHOOT STRAIGHT

You'll like our work. Or maybe your next pair of shoes will come from a cement mixer.
Weddings, bar mitzvahs, rich kids' birthday parties and great ads. Call us.

Detroit, Mich. (313) 868-2200 • Atlanta, Ga. (404) 355-5271 • Pittsburgh, Pa. (412) 261-1444 • London, England 0140-70909 Telex 888607 • Los Angeles, Cal. (213) 659-5315

From Left to Right: Glen Daly, John Wisner, Tammy Benson, Joe Higgins, Bob Traniello, Jimmy Northmore, Gary Ryan, Mickey McGuire, Jerry Bojarski, Mason Pawlak
Photo: Jimmy Northmore • Lettering: Lettering, Inc. • Printing: Service Engraving • Type: Willens • Design: Bob Folster • Copy: Bob Bonin • Clothes: Tim Dewart

THE GANG THAT CONTINUED TO SHOOT AND PROSPER
When this promotional poster was made, Boulevard's expanding empire included offices in Detroit, Atlanta, Pittsburgh, Los Angeles, *and* London.

With Hartwell headlining the show and Northmore acting as his assistant—as well as running the darkroom and lab facilities—New Center Photographic's business grew steadily. In short order, it was in need of more help, which would arrive in the form of Mickey McGuire.

Soon after starting his servitude with Clark, McGuire had gotten married. "My wife and I both worked," he explained. "She was making about $60 a week, and after a couple of years I was up to maybe $35. Still, we were doing fine until the wrong one got pregnant." With that, McGuire really had to scurry, taking pictures of weddings and anything else that would earn some extra money. But it wasn't enough, so he gathered up samples of his automotive work and, as he says, "went down the street to New Center Photographic, where I met Jimmy Northmore and became another of Cliff Hartwell's assistants and flunkies."

All went well for another year or so, but then, in the words of McGuire, "Cliff Hartwell started to get old and crabby." At the same time, Greenwald began thinking that it might be time to get out of the advertising business and into something simpler—something that might give him a better return on his investment. His idea was that New Center Photographic should go into the business of making slide films. (Slide-film presentations were quite the rage in the 1950s and 1960s. They were made up of individual color transparencies on continuous strips of film that could be projected onto a screen, sometimes accompanied by an audiotape that "beeped" when it was time to advance to the next frame.)

To Greenwald, the making and duplication of these things seemed like the perfect way to make use of the many facets of his business. One day he told McGuire and Northmore that's what he intended to do. They, however, found the idea laughably pedestrian and didn't take the boss seriously until the next day. That's when Greenwald announced that since they weren't interested in making slide films, he was putting the studio up for sale, and if someone didn't buy it, he was going to close the place up. He would, however, consider an employee buyout. He was asking $125,000, but would take 10 percent down, with the balance due over the course of 10 years. Without other jobs to go to, it was an offer that Northmore says "we couldn't refuse." The only problem was raising the down payment. Fortunately, John Hoppin, one of the studio's salesmen, was also interested in becoming a partner. Thus, a three-way deal was struck. In 1954, after each scraped together $4,000, McGuire, Northmore, and Hoppin acquired the debts and assets of New Center Photographic.

The question now was what to call this new enterprise. The partners considered clever combinations of their own names, but eventually decided to follow the example set by Greenwald, who believed that a name on the door was less important than the work that comes out of it. Because the studio was located on East Grand Boulevard in Detroit, they decided the company might as well be Boulevard Photographic.

HIGH TIMES IN MONACO
The 1973 Arab oil embargo was a rude awakening for U. S. car makers and for Boulevard. The year before, big cars, expensive shoots, and exotic locations were in. The next year they were all out.

AFTER THE STORM

When the Arab embargo upset the status quo in 1973, McGuire and Northmore faced some anxious moments. However, as evidenced by this gag shot taken after wrapping-up a Ford shoot in the early 1980s, they would utimately survive and prosper. Here, members of the crew and J. Walter Thompson art director, Larry Kosiba (center), pay homage to Northmore (right) and a piece of his then newly patented "motion rig" which helped bring in riches from traditional domestic and new imported car clients alike.

This turned out to be one of the few things that the partners would actually agree upon.

Although both Northmore and McGuire credit Hoppin with playing a key role in their early success, philosophically they never quite saw eye-to-eye. Hoppin was about ten years their senior, and despite being partners, his view was that McGuire and Northmore worked for him. Things went from bad to worse, and in a couple of years they decided that either he or they had to go. McGuire says, "Jimmy and I figured out what the company was worth, and we went to John and said, 'You can buy us out for this amount, or we'll buy you out—it's your choice.'" Hoppin chose the latter, bid Boulevard adieu, and later realized great success in a totally unrelated field: the mobile-home-park business.

Despite any differences that McGuire and Northmore might have had with John Hoppin, they never questioned the importance of selling

CELEBRATING ITS PROUD PAST

With as many cars as Boulevard would shoot over the years, it was never short of examples for making sample sheets like this, which were regularly sent to art directors and clients.

and salespeople. Indeed, among the many things that distinguished them as "artists" was their willingness and ability to effectively sell their work. They were also aware that they couldn't do everything themselves, so they made a point of hiring the best salespeople.

One of the first people to come to work for Boulevard was, in fact, a salesman named Bud Hassard. He started in the days of John Hoppin and stayed with Boulevard throughout its existence. Another one of Boulevard's earliest and longest-serving salespeople was Dick Crandall. He was the boyhood friend who was along on the vacation trip to Mackinaw Island that originally led Northmore to New Center Studio. Crandall left an engineering job with General Motors to join Boulevard

in its early days and stayed for the duration. Boulevard always depended on excellent salespeople. In fact, in later years, two salesmen—Jack Weber and Pat Costa—would become part owners of the company.

As a business, Boulevard Photographic was built and survived on long-standing relationships. Just months after the business was incorporated, a young man named Walter "Wally" Sternicki came to work in the studio. He, too, never left. Sternicki worked side by side with McGuire throughout his entire career. He became McGuire's alter ego, worrying about the equipment, which allowed Mickey to focus on the pictures. When it came to McGuire's camera and equipment, Sternicki was like a well-trained infantryman who knows how to assemble and disassemble his rifle in the dark. Another of Boulevard's longest-serving and most valued employees was Millie Kelly. She started out as a model working for Cliff Hartwell in the days before Boulevard was officially founded. Millie, however, was more than just a pretty face, and went on to serve as Boulevard's coordinator of models, fashion, and locations.

Although Northmore and McGuire were always the heart and soul of Boulevard Photographic, they were by no means the company's only photographers. Both took immense pride in their work and were driven by competitive as well as creative urges, but self-aggrandizement wasn't the reason they'd gotten into the business. Their objective was to satisfy the photographic needs of the automotive industry. And when demand outpaced what they could reasonably handle themselves, they didn't hesitate to train and employ other photographers to deliver the Boulevard look, style, and quality. Boulevard's roster could include more than a dozen name photographers at one time, many of whom started out as assistants working primarily with Northmore. Over the years, Boulevard became, quite literally, a school of photography, spreading its art and magic worldwide. Many of the best known and most influential car shooters worked or trained at Boulevard. Veteran car photographer Guy Morrison worked with McGuire and Northmore in the early days. Later alumnae included the likes of Robert Traniello, Dennis Wiand, Joe Higgins, Ken Stidwell, Glenn Daly, Doug Taub, John Wisner, and Peggy Day.

As the demand for Boulevard's work grew, so too did the need for bigger and more technically sophisticated facilities. Right from the start, Northmore and McGuire routinely found themselves renting and shooting in places like the Detroit National Guard Armory. This was because the studio on East Grand Boulevard—which they'd taken over from New Center Photographic—simply wasn't big enough or tall enough to handle a lot of jobs. In 1960, they finally left their company's namesake behind and moved into a brand new, state-of-the-art facility on a street known simply as "Victor" in Highland Park, on Detroit's north side. For this building, McGuire acted as the architect, while Northmore came up with the building's key features, which not only included vast floor space and a soaring, 30-foot-tall ceiling, but things like a crow's nest to facilitate down shots, an overhead structure to handle lighting flats, rolling walls, offices, and lab facilities. This, however, would be just the first in what would eventually become five studios and buildings known as Boulevard's Victor complex.

When it came to acquiring or developing equipment and facilities, McGuire and Northmore refused to play second fiddle to anyone. This included General Motors' giant photographic division and its long-time head, Walter Farynk, who was also a pioneer and one of he true legends in the field of automotive photography. For example, before the advent of digital imaging and "blue-screen" matting the movie industry came up with a system called "front-screen projection" to simulate outdoor backgrounds when shooting on interior sound stages. Such systems were complicated and extraordinarily expensive, but when word got out that Farynk had installed one at GM Photographic, McGuire and Northmore decided Boulevard should have one too. They found that the front-screen projection system could be employed to create abstract and artistic backgrounds that couldn't be found in nature. For most projects, however, they found it was usually cheaper and easier to shoot on location.

Shooting cars for advertising was a highly seasonal business. Historically, car makers tended to all introduce their new models at the same time. Multiple stages and studios allowed Boulevard to handle the work of a number of clients at once, while maintaining the kind of security that was often essential. As might be expected, manufacturers insisted on keeping their prototypes and new models under wraps and away from the prying eyes of the public and competitors. To keep an operation of this size going, Boulevard needed a sizable support staff.

With unrivaled facilities, personnel, and equipment, Boulevard dominated the field of automotive photography in ways that individual photographers working alone could not. At one time or another, it's been estimated that Boulevard was doing three-quarters of all the photography used in automotive advertising and promotion. Even so, they weren't the only game in town. Photographers such as Dennis Gripentrog, Vern Hammarlund, and Warren Winstanley may not have been able to compete in terms of volume, but McGuire and Northmore never took them lightly. Winstanley, in particular, was one photographer McGuire considered an inspiration as well as a competitor.

Although Detroit was always the center of its universe, Boulevard's activities expanded nationally and internationally. To

ENJOY video-taped documentaries that EXPLORE the working world of these OUTSTANDING photographers...

BOULEVARD **B**PHOTOGRAPHIC

Veteran automobile photographer, Mickey McGuire, highlights several controls and tricks of the trade that can help *you* turn out better commercial photography. Pre-touching versus retouching, natural versus artificial lighting, special effects, and how to work with assistants are only some of the secrets he'll share.

Jimmy Northmore may shoot cars in the studio, but they look like they're racing down the highway! A special motion rig helps him create the effect, and really helps the photos sell. In this year's Visions in View program, Jimmy describes the machine in detail and also gives sound advice on how you can foster good business with clients and good relations with ad agencies.

THE BOULEVARD SCHOOL OF PHOTOGRAPHY
above and right
While more than a few photographers got on-the-job training at Boulevard, countless others were able to learn from the masters thanks to Kodak's *Vision in View* videotapes and articles in publications including *Applied Photography.*

better serve clients outside of the Motor City, Boulevard opened and operated studios in Pittsburgh, Atlanta, and Los Angeles. In the late 1960s, Europeans also demanded the services of Boulevard. Up until then, European manufacturers had relied upon conservative, matter-of-fact photographs to sell cars. The Boulevard look and style contrasted sharply with the approach of most European photographers. As McGuire likes to say, "We introduced Europeans to sex and romance at least as far as car advertising is concerned." Eventually, there was enough work to warrant an operation with a full-time photographer

CORPORATE EFFICIENCY

Like Northmore, McGuire developed an affinity for airplanes and would own a series of airplanes, the last of which was a pressurized-cabin Cessna 421 Golden Eagle with personalized "N" number, 35MM. It not only facilitated McGuire's commutes from his home in Palm Springs, California, it was also handy as a background prop.

stationed in Europe. Joe Higgins, a talented young photographer who started out as Northmore's assistant, spearheaded Boulevard's European assault. Higgins' work set Europe on fire. With studios in Düsseldorf and London, Boulevard International eventually became the biggest supplier of car photography in Europe. Even Northmore and McGuire regularly found themselves going abroad, shooting for a variety of companies in far-flung locations such as Cyprus, Portugal, Spain, Switzerland, and Germany.

As a result of being so dependent upon the car business, when the automobile industry sneezed, Boulevard could catch a cold. When the oil embargo hit in October 1973—triggering a recession and focusing attention on fuel-efficient cars—Boulevard Photographic was nearly devastated. The effect was put into perspective by Wally Sternicki, "In 1972, we were shooting big cars and basking in Monaco, and the next spring we were all wondering if we were going to have jobs."

The BUSINESS of BOULEVARD 3

THE future of photography may have appeared bright when Jimmy Northmore and Mickey McGuire decided to take up Art Greenwald on his offer to sell New Center Photographic, but in the words of Northmore, "In the beginning, we had to struggle just to get enough business to keep the place from collapsing financially."

Although photography could offer credibility, artists could still do things that photographers couldn't—particularly when it came to embellishing the style or proportions of a vehicle. What's more, the photographic materials available at the time—particularly color transparency films—were extremely unpredictable and difficult to work with. As a result, art directors may have been willing to look at photography, but actually getting jobs was an uphill battle.

CHOOSING BOULEVARD

After a somewhat rocky start in the late 1950s, Boulevard and the Ford Motor Company would enjoy a mutually profitable relationship. Including domestic and overseas assignments, Ford became Boulevard's biggest and best account.

THE BUSINESS OF BOULEVARD

In an effort to control everything that goes into an automobile, car companies have been known to go so far as to mine their own iron ore and smelt their own steel. Given this, one might logically assume that they'd certainly want to make their own ads. The truth is, however, that though ads and commercials bear a car maker's imprints and logos, they are, with rare exceptions, the products of an advertising agency.

That otherwise self-sufficient companies would choose to let outsiders handle their advertising is not new nor is it unique to the automobile industry. The practice actually goes back to the middle of the nineteenth century when the miracles of mass production first began to require companies to advertise on an ever-increasing basis as they sought new and ever-bigger markets. Advertising thus became a valuable commodity, which gave rise to the first advertising agents, who acted primarily as brokers.

For a fee or commission, these enterprising souls undertook to find publications in which companies could advertise, kept track of circulations, negotiated rates, and then bought "space" on behalf of their clients. Initially, agents cared little about what occupied the space they bought, but this would change as their clients began to judge the value of advertising not just on what it cost, but in terms of how many sales it delivered. And as competition for lucrative commissions increased, the most successful agents and agencies would be those who were not only shrewd buyers, but also gifted salesman, able to create ads of proven effectiveness and sell their services as indispensable.

It thus came to pass that companies that deigned to do their own advertising ran the risk of appearing like the lawyer who has himself for a client. In other words, a fool, which explains why not even Henry Ford's vertically integrated business model included making ads "in-house." Therefore, the people Jimmy Northmore and

Nash Presents America's Newest Hardtop Convertible
The Rambler "Country Club"

NASH RAMBLER COUNTRY CLUB
Nash was one of the first postwar converts to photography. In the beginning, its art directors sought to use photographs in a photojournalistic style, using many pictures to tell a product story.

Mickey McGuire first had to sell on photography weren't car companies, but rather the art directors at the auto makers' advertising agencies.

The good news was that the postwar environment encouraged risk takers. The production of new civilian automobiles had been suspended for the better part of four and a half years during the war, and demand for new cars after the war was extraordinary. Slowed by the process of reorganizing and retooling before they could resume production, the "Big Three"—GM, Ford, and Chrysler—were unable to immediately satisfy the market. This gave companies that had been minor players or nonexistent before the war, an opportunity to make hay. In fact, the independents' share of the market climbed to 50 percent before the Big Three got their houses in order and started reversing the trend in 1950. And it was the agencies and art directors working for the "upstarts" and "independents" who gave McGuire and Northmore their first major breaks. And of these, none were more important than Odie James and John MacClure, art directors on the Nash account.

When the war ended, Nash was able to resume production more quickly than most. Like many of its rivals, Nash's initial offerings were warmed-over prewar models. However, Nash's prewar designs were more modern than most, and the company profited handsomely in the immediate postwar years. This success gave Nash the wherewithal to develop a new type of car that Nash President George Mason hoped would establish a new segment. In 1950, the year after Nash introduced its new big cars—the "Airflyte" Ambassadors and 600s—it debuted what was to be the prototype for postwar compacts, the Rambler. While the little Ramblers borrowed the bathtub styling from their bigger siblings, they were designed for buyers interested in economy and practicality. To distinguish the

PHOTOGRAPHY GAVE ART DIRECTORS SOMETHING TO DIRECT

Photography allowed art directors to get directly involved in the making of pictures. Here, Nash art director Odie James (center) is on the scene as Northmore (right) directs the shot and assistant Wally Sternicki (left) opens the shutter.

A CAR FOR ALL REASONS

Billed as the world's safest convertible and high-mileage champ, Nash also wanted to show that the Rambler was at home at the country club.

ALL IN THE FAMILY

Advertising sometimes showed more than products. After Hudson and Nash were amalgamated to form the American Motors Corporation (AMC) in 1954, the similar look and style of Nash and Hudson ads reflected their corporate kinship.

THROUGH THE LOOKING GLASS
In 1963, small cars and fuel economy were not things people took very seriously. So the objective was to make the economical Rambler American look like fun.

Rambler from the competition and to communicate its virtues credibly, James and MacClure decided a break with tradition was in order, leading them to photography and to McGuire and Northmore. MacClure gave them their major assignments shooting Rambler brochures, which proved to be a rousing success. MacClure and James would go on to become regular clients, sticking with Boulevard for many years, through the days of both Nash and American Motors.

Kaiser was another of the independents who sought to strike while postwar demand for cars was hot. Henry J. Kaiser was a colorful California businessman who'd risen to national prominence during World War II as an ingenious and prolific producer of war materiel, particularly ships. During the war, he joined forces with Joseph W. Frazer,

then president of the Graham-Paige Motor Company, with a plan to enter into large-scale automobile production at the war's end.

Kaiser was both an entrepreneur and an opportunist and managed to lease and buy surplus war plants for next to nothing—it's reported that he even got $44 million from the government to finance his purchases. Kaiser began production of passenger cars right after the war, initially doing very well. When Americans began to show a fondness for sports cars, he decided to make his own, the 1954 Kaiser Darrin 161. It was an unorthodox design with novel features such as sliding doors and a landau-style convertible top roof. The introduction of Darrin was also somewhat unorthodox. Instead of handing the project off to an ad agency, Kaiser engaged the services of a sports car enthusiast-turned-PR-man named Jim Wangers.

MAKING THE RIDICULOUS SUBLIME
AMC was not only a steady source of business, it was also the source for some of the weirdest and most unusual cars to ever find their way into Boulevard's studios, including, but not limited to, this wicker-sided Gremlin and faux-wood-sided Pacer wagon.

Knowing that the dreams and desires of sports car enthusiasts like himself were fueled by the photographs that appeared in magazines like *Road & Track*, Wangers naturally gravitated toward use of photography. However, he also intuited that the Darrin would only stand out if the photography stood out from the usual editorial fare. Thus, Wangers found his way to Northmore and McGuire who rolled a Darrin into the studio where they lavished it with proper light and attention.

Unfortunately, Kaiser fortunes began to crumble, and the Darrin was abandoned after just one year. Fewer than 450 Darrins were sold. Though the car wasn't much of a success, the dramatic black-and-white photography of McGuire and Northmore was. The catalog earned them their first industry awards. It also helped launch the career of Wangers, who went on to become a master automotive public-relations man, and later played a major role in successfully launching another "oddball" car, the Pontiac GTO.

ANGLING FOR A FISH
McGuire found that shooting AMC's Marlin from this angle hid the fact that it had started out as a Rambler. It thus became the view shown in ads. Unfortunately, there was no way to keep people from seeing the ungainly Marlin from other angles once they got to the showroom, helping to explain why it only lasted three years (1965–1967).

Just before Art Greenwald decided to get out of the photography business, he invited art directors and other clients to a show staged inside the "tent" of New Center's photo studio. One of those in attendance was Mack Stanley, an art director on the Packard account. He was impressed with the facilities and with Northmore and McGuire. As a result, he gave them a chance to do some experimental work in an attempt to sell Packard on the use of photography and tent lighting. This led to the 1954 Packard catalogs and advertising, which featured cars photographed inside the "tent," with backgrounds designed by the noted New York fashion artist René Bouché.

Mack Stanley continued to be a big supporter and regular Boulevard client. After the demise of Packard, he would move on to make his mark on other automotive accounts, including Oldsmobile, taking Boulevard along for the ride. Usually dressing in black and affecting either black derby hat or beret, Stanley was an eccentric character. And although he had a penchant for unusual ideas, he was also a staunch advocate of using a consistent look and theme to tie together a whole year's ads and catalogs.

Using backgrounds and models always held great appeal to Stanley. At the end of his career, he and Jimmy Northmore teamed up to create a series of three particularly unusual and memorable campaigns for Oldsmobile, starting in 1968. The first was based on a concept that

AVANT GARDE

With a landau-style roof that approximated a sort of targa top, sliding doors, and a fiberglass body, Howard "Dutch" Darrin's radical Kaiser sports car was perhaps too far ahead of its time in 1954. Although it failed in the marketplace, it afforded Northmore and McGuire a catalog and advertising assignment that earned them industry notoriety and awards.

Kaiser·Darrin **161**

A new criterion of motoring performance

a new standard of luxury.

44

INSIDE THE TENT

Mack Stanley, an art director on the Packard account, was quick to see the advantages of tent lighting and commissioned Northmore and McGuire to shoot Packard catalogs and advertising even before Boulevard was officially incorporated. This 1954 Packard limo was just one in a series of shots made inside the tent, with backgrounds by noted fashion illustrator, René Bouché.

Jimmy had originally conceived for Chevrolet. It involved double-exposing scenes of people engaged in youthful activities into shots of cars photographed in the studio. The next year's campaign again dealt with multiple images, but it was even more ambitious. The idea was to portray Oldsmobiles in the context of classic movie stars and themes. Recreating the old-time movie scenes that were made into billboard-size blowups for the backgrounds called for some very elaborate staging and shooting. For the third and last in this series of multiple-image campaigns, Oldsmobiles were photographed in front of different tableaux—using props and models—to link the cars to the everyday experiences of various buyers.

Fred Peck, an art director on the Dodge account, was another client who played a key role in Boulevard's early success and in advancing the use of photography in advertising. In search of "white chrome," he'd used Boulevard's tent studio for Dodge's 1955 advertising. He liked the results, but didn't like the limitations imposed by the tent. As Stanley had done the year before on Packard, Peck had used models and painted backgrounds to add interest to the 1955 Dodge photography. For 1956, Peck wanted out of the studio. Thus, if Northmore and McGuire intended to keep him as a customer, they needed to recreate the look of studio lighting outside. The problem, as McGuire is fond of saying, was that "when the sun is in God's beautiful blue sky, you're going to get blue chrome." He and Northmore found they could avoid the problem by merely shooting under overcast skies, but it wasn't always practical to sit around and wait for cloudy days. So Jimmy suggested going to the San Francisco Bay Area where days typically started out with fog and overcast. Peck was game to try it. Thus, he and Northmore headed west.

For several weeks they traveled through California, taking "test" photographs of borrowed cars in various locations with the intent of showing the results to the agency and client, then returning to re-shoot the new 1956 model-year vehicles. The experiment worked, and for 1956 much of Dodge's brochure and ad work was shot on the West Coast.

MACK STANLEY

Mack Stanley (second from right) was an eccentric character as well as an excellent Boulevard client. Through the years, he would be the man behind many of Boulevard's biggest and most challenging assignments.

MORE CLEANUP THAN SETUP

Perhaps because of this Packard ad, shot by Northmore in front of the National Art Museum in Washington D.C., Stanley developed a preference for working in the studio. After the shooting was completed, it was necessary to steam clean and polish the gallery's marble walk because the elegant Packard had been inelegantly leaking oil.

Peck became a very adventuresome user of photography. In 1957 he went so far as to create a series of Dodge ads that appeared without headlines. He decided to let the picture "tell the story." The ads garnered a lot of attention with the public and in the advertising community, which voted them many awards. Peck went on to become one of Boulevard's steadiest customers, working primarily with Northmore into the 1960s. His interest in pushing the bounds of photography also helped inspire both McGuire and Northmore to come up with ever-better ideas, such as using overhead or "flying" lighting flats in lieu of the "tent," and their novel curved film holders, which first allowed them to stretch cars like an artist.

Even so, Peck was known to occasionally give Northmore and McGuire a start. In the spring of 1956, he informed them that Dodge was considering a return to artwork for 1957. Like Chrysler's other divisions, the 1957 Dodges would feature radical new styling. Dodge's "swept-wing" look was particularly extreme, and it was feared that it might not play well in photographs. From a financial standpoint, this could have been a major setback to the still fledgling business. So Northmore and McGuire breathed a sigh of relief when Pontiac appeared with a problem that Boulevard might be able to solve.

While Peck worried that the look of the 1957 Dodges might be too extreme, over at Pontiac the concerns were just the opposite.

A wild-blue-yonder kind of excitement: Olds Cutlass S.

Run-of-the-mill cars got you feeling grounded? Spread your wings and soar in a Cutlass S. Rocket 350 V-8 (or big 250 Action-Line Six), louvered hood,

hideaway wipers, new GM safety features, standard.
Want to really send the ordinary into a tailspin? Order yours with bucket seats, center

console, and G.T. hood stripes. Price? Right down your runway. Every Olds Cutlass sports an easy-to-take low price. **Escape from the ordinary.**

NOW SHOWING YOUNGMOBILE THINKING 1969

STANLEY CAMPAIGNS

A believer in the strength of continuity, Mack Stanley always sought a unifying look for his ads and catalogs. These are examples of three Oldsmobile campaigns that ran consecutively from 1968 through 1970. The theme for each year may have been different, but all of them relied on multiple images to position the cars.

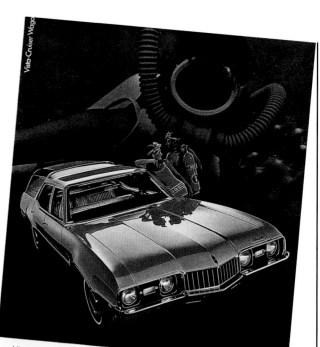

Vista-Cruiser: Whopping new Youngmobile wagon. For '68, even bigger than ever to carry more of the things you carry. Two seats or three, all facing front. Plus a 350-cubic-inch Rocket V-8—up to 400 cubic inches big!

STARTING IN THE STUDIO

In search of "white chrome," Dodge art director Fred Peck also found his way to Boulevard's tent studio. Though pleased with the results, he quickly realized that "tent pictures" tended to all look alike.

The reality was that styling was not exactly a strong point for 1957. Its agency's art directors were looking for some way to perk up Pontiac's ads without focusing too much attention on its cars. Hearing of Pontiac's plight, Northmore and McGuire came up with an idea. They suggested that showing people jumping for joy in Pontiac's ads might provide a kind of happy distraction. Pontiac liked the idea and gave them the assignment. As it turned out, Peck would ultimately change his mind, and he used photography in the majority of Dodge's advertising in 1957—which was more good news for Boulevard.

It's interesting to note that when GM's divisions introduced their radically restyled cars in 1959, their advertising people would find themselves pondering the same question—whether to go with photography or art? Initially, most decided to stick with art, perhaps because the 1959 styling was extreme enough to warrant a certain amount of softening by the artist's hand. And although photography would eventually find its way back into most GM advertising, Pontiac would stick with artwork for more than a decade. After introducing the "wide-track" look with artwork in 1959, Pontiac made use of illustrations through 1971.

Another of Boulevard's most stalwart clients was Bob Dunning, art director on the Plymouth account. In 1960, he came up with an idea that involved using the same two models, with hair dyed silver, in all of the pictures. Boulevard's relationship with Dunning also involved a great deal of location photography. For 1961, he wanted lots of "snapshot"-like pictures for use in the Plymouth catalogs. He also wanted to show Plymouths and people in many different locations— Smoky Mountains, New York, Florida, and so forth. This called for a number of long, location trips, during which hundreds of pictures were shot.

To get a candid feel in the photographs, Northmore suggested using a 2-1/4-inch single-lens-reflex camera instead of the usual 8x10-inch, and shooting everything on color negative film, which would mean reproducing from prints. It had never been tried before, but it seemed like it ought to work. It did, but it wasn't easy. Northmore quickly discovered that the color print film was pretty crude, grainy, and very unstable. On top of that, when shooting was finished, all you had to show the client were contact sheets or rough black-and-white proofs.

Historically, the advertising business has not been known for loyalty—campaigns change from one season to the next, agencies are fired for fluctuations in sales, photographers come and go according to what's hot or trendy. The departure of an agency art director could spell disaster for companies like Boulevard. When Fred Peck left the automobile advertising business and was replaced by Jim Hanna, Northmore and McGuire fully expected that it would be the end of their Dodge business. To the contrary, Hanna, a newcomer to Detroit and to car photography, relied heavily upon Boulevard. Hanna

The Success Car of the Year . . . dramatically beautiful, dynamically powered.

A new world of adventure is waiting for you

DISCOVER THE DIFFERENCE IN DODGE !

Has it occurred to you that there are some things you've been *missing* because you haven't found time to *discover the difference* in Dodge?

The difference is there—and it's wonderful!

It starts with styling so fresh and new that you experience a lift in your spirits every time you step into your new Dodge. The sweep of soaring Jet Fins is an invitation to adventure.

Then there's the ease and safety of Dodge "Magic Touch" push-button driving—sure, safe, positive control right at your fingertips.

You discover a new kind of power . . . surging *break-away* power from the Super Red Ram V-8 that blazed

a trail of records on the Bonneville Salt Flats *no other car* has ever equalled.

There's a world of difference in the *feel* of Dodge *full-size* power steering, the *feel* of Dodge Safe-Guard power brakes, the *feel* of the gliding Oriflow ride that adjusts automatically to every road condition.

It's all different—the *bigness* of this new Dodge, the roominess and comfort that actually exceeds cars costing a thousand dollars more.

Won't you take time *this week* to discover the wonderful difference in Dodge? It can all be yours in the superb Coronet Series—full-size, full-styled, full-powered—yet priced right down with the "low price field." It's your biggest buy—by far!

New '56
DODGE

➤ *VALUE LEADER OF THE FORWARD LOOK*

Dodge Dealers present Danny Thomas in "Make Room for Daddy," Bert Parks in "Break the Bank," The Lawrence Welk Show—all on ABC-TV

This is your reward for the great Dodge advance—the daring new, dramatic new '56 Dodge.

The Magic Touch of Tomorrow!

The *look* of success! The *feel* of success! The *power* of success!

They come to you in a dramatically beautiful, dynamically powered new Dodge that introduces the ease and safety of push-button driving —the Magic Touch of Tomorrow! It is a truly great value.

New '56 DODGE

➤ *VALUE LEADER OF THE FORWARD LOOK*

GOING OUTSIDE

For 1956, Peck and Northmore ventured to the San Francisco Bay Area where they found interesting locations, and where foggy morning skies yielded "natural" tent lighting. However, the most notable feature of the 1956 Dodge advertising was its emphasis on tail fins.

turned out to be one of Boulevard's best customers, keeping the studios occupied shooting work for things like the hugely popular "Dodge Rebellion" campaigns of the late 1960s.

Of all the accounts that McGuire and Northmore served, none was bigger or more important to Boulevard than Ford. Yet, this relationship got off to a somewhat rocky start.

Starting in 1955, Ford's agency, J. Walter Thompson, had engaged McGuire for a number of one-off assignments that led to him landing the job as the lead photographer for what was slated to be Ford's 1957 national advertising campaign. The theme was to be

"proved and approved around the world," and the agency had come up with the idea of linking this "global" concept to the large, round taillights of Ford's 1957 models. This, of course, meant shooting all of the cars from the rear, which was extremely unusual, but McGuire figured the agency people knew what they were doing. It was a massive shoot, involving elaborate sets and high-paid fashion models from the Eileen Ford modeling agency. Despite its complexity, everything went without a hitch, and McGuire completed the assignment much to the delight of the agency. Unfortunately, the people at Ford had not approved the concept, refused to pay for

DETROIT AUTOMOBILE CIRCLES are buzzing about the buying surge to the new "Swept-Wing" Dodge. Car is 4½ feet low on a big 122" wheelbase, powered by unique aircraft-type engine rated up to 310 hp. Autodynamic advances include revolutionary suspension system (Torsion-Aire) which virtually eliminates road-sway and brake-dip, isolates vibration. Driver controls all speed ranges of new transmission by push button. Lowest-priced model of Dodge line is selling in Detroit for $2165, including taxes. Others up to $3600. Dodge president, M. C. (Matt) Patterson, sums up spectacular sales this way: "Every 45 seconds somebody 'joins the swing to Swept-Wing' and buys a new Dodge." The new car is currently on display at local Dodge dealers.

LET THE PICTURE DO THE TALKING

As an art director, Peck believed in the power of pictures to tell a story. This 1957 Dodge ad was one in a series he designed that featured photographs unfettered by headlines.

A BIT OF A STRETCH

In addition to ideal lighting, Peck also sought idealized proportions. This ad made use of Boulevard's novel stretch film holders to accentuate the length of the Dodge's "Swept-Wing" styling for 1957.

the shoot, and wanted to know whose dumb idea it was to shoot tail-lights. McGuire was not there to answer, so he got the credit. And as a result, Boulevard was pretty much off the list for J. Walter Thompson's art directors for several years until a new creative regime came to power, headed by Andy Nelson.

Under the guidance of Nelson, J. Walter Thompson's art directors would engage McGuire and Northmore to do some of their most inventive work. This came about in large part because Nelson believed in commissioning experimental photography—not just for the purposes of previewing an idea—but as a means of generating new ones. Nelson constantly challenged McGuire and Northmore to stretch the photographic envelope. And although they would sometimes complain that their best stuff didn't always turn up in Ford ads, the Ford account would ultimately become Boulevard's biggest.

Boulevard also did work for other Ford divisions. Thanks to Lincoln-Mercury and its agency, Kenyon & Eckhardt, McGuire and Northmore were introduced to another group of art directors, which included the likes of Jonas Gold, Rocco Campanelli, and a couple characters named Walter Granberg and Paul Levy. Northmore worked primarily with Granberg, while McGuire worked more with Levy, but both were capable of coming up with challenging assignments, particularly when it came to using animals.

One memorable Kenyon & Eckhardt animal campaign was for the Mercury Comet. It appeared in the early 1960s and starred a giant sheep dog named Boo. Attempts to get this shaggy hound to hold still, much less strike a pose, were generally exercises in futility. Boo, however, was somewhat easier to deal

WHY ARE THESE PEOPLE JUMPING?

For 1957, Pontiac's conservative styling put it out of phase with current trends. Afraid that its cars alone would fail to generate excitement, Pontiac's agency called on Boulevard for help.

NO EXAGGERATION NECESSARY

With the introduction of the 283-cubic-inch version of Chevrolet's small-block V-8, the availability of Rochester fuel injection, and up to 283 horsepower, the Corvette became a legitimate performance car in 1957, a fact emphasized by this straightforward, no-nonsense portrayal. Throughout the years, the mission of Corvette advertising has remained remarkably consistent as this 1984 ad shows.

ALWAYS SEARCHING FOR AN IDENTITY

Plymouth Art Director Bob Dunning would engage Boulevard in many different types of assignments. As these three samples show, Plymouth advertising could include extravagant studio techniques, outdoor beauty shots, and even prophetic black-and-white images.

with than the cougar named Chauncey who later appeared in Mercury Cougar ads. It was thought that Chauncey could be induced to do anything if plied with enough raw chicken necks, but this did not include letting someone paint racing stripes down his back for a picture.

In 1978, Lee Iacocca took over the reigns of the Chrysler Corporation after being unceremoniously let go from the Ford Motor Company. During his years with Ford, Iacocca had developed a close relationship with Kenyon & Eckhardt. In 1980, Iacocca convinced Kenyon & Eckhardt to resign the Lincoln-Mercury account and take over the Chrysler Corporation's adver-

tising. Kenyon & Eckhardt art directors thus inherited a whole new set of problems and advertising objectives.

At the time, there may have been those who wondered if Chrylser was going to make it, but there was no longer any question of the viability of photography or the talents of McGuire and Northmore. Kenyon & Eckhardt art directors called upon them to help launch the new Chrysler Corporation, while the art directors at Lincoln-Mercury's new agency counted on them as well.

McGuire and Northmore were able to establish themselves, photography, and Boulevard Photographic because they were able to meet the ever-changing rules and players in the automotive

CORPORATE CONFIDENCE

Over the years, Boulevard did work for all of Chrysler's divisions, which of course included Chrysler and Imperial. At times, the distinctions between the corporation's two top nameplates were difficult to discern.

industry. As such, Boulevard's roster of clients came to include imported as well as domestic nameplates. When Japanese automakers entered the market, many would find their way to Boulevard Photographic. The likes of Datsun and Toyota quickly determined that while energy concerns, consumerism, and changing lifestyles may have opened the door, being welcome required presenting themselves in American images and terms.

By contrast, when European cars appeared in America, the agencies that represented them were inclined to eschew the services of Boulevard Photographic. Even when Boulevard photography became a hot commodity in car advertising in Europe, Europeans

doing business in America wanted to avoid anything that smacked of domestic fare, and that included Boulevard Photographic. One notable exception was an art director named Marce Mayhew who, in the late 1970s, came to preside over the sagging fortunes of England's British Leyland group of cars, which included MG, Triumph, Rover, and Jaguar. After the first three "failed to proceed," as the British would say, Mayhew guided Jaguar through a resurrection and resurgence during the 1980s. In doing so, he relied heavily on Northmore and McGuire to bring Jaguar images to life.

When McGuire and Northmore started out, they, like photography itself, were unknown commodities. Their first clients came from

GIVE YOURSELF A BIG BRAKE! Coronet '66 brakes match up perfectly with Coronet power! Big, safe, dependable . . . and self-adjusting, too.

TACH* . . . GO! Coronet 500's floor stick puts control right at hand. TorqueFlite automatic* (or 4-speed stick)* comes console-mounted.
*Optional at extra cost.

STICK . . . on Coronet 500 center console.

MORE FANG—LESS FUSS. "225" stands for the Six that sizzles. "383" stands for the 4-barrel V8 that snarls. In between: 3 other great V8s!

MOST-OFTEN-SEEN VIEW OF CORONET '66—pulling away from other cars. Proves that Coronet '66 looks great from every angle. Proves another point: Low trunk sill makes luggage loading easy. Even the spare tire has its own special storage well under the flat trunk floor. With so much "go" up front—and so much "stow" in back—better join the Rebellion and go traveling in Coronet '66!

THE DODGE REBELLION

Dodge was always a big part of Boulevard's business. And the "Dodge Rebellion" played a large role in establishing Dodge as Chrysler's most feisty division. The centerpiece of the campaign, which covered all models, was the "Dodge girls." They commanded as much, if not more, space and attention in ads and brochures as did the cars.

ENTER THE BIG BORE HUNTER

Dodge Coronet R/T... with 440-Magnum

Drag fans, here's your car. Coronet R/T packs 440 cubic inches of go! The big-inch, deep-breathing 440-Magnum sports a special 4-barrel carburetor, larger exhaust valves, longer duration cam and low-restriction dual exhaust. Underneath there's a heavy-duty

suspension with sway bar and special shock absorbers for better handling, high-performance nylon cord Red Streak tires, and big 3-inch-wide brakes—front and rear—for surer stops. Front disc brakes are optional. An extra leaf in the right rear spring copes with torque and helps prevent

wheel hop. Coronet R/T comes on strong with sizzling style, too. Body side paint stripes, distinctive hood air-scoop design, bucket front seats, and special R/T insignia put it lengths ahead of the look-alike crowd. Hunting for trophy-winning performance that handles

beautifully on the road? Check the odds. They're 440 to 1 in favor of Coronet R/T . . . a balanced automobile engineered for the enthusiast.

"Dodge Rebellion Operation '67 Wants You"

Dodge

the ranks of the upstarts, independents, and also-rans. In short order, however, art directors from everywhere were lining up to use the photography and services of Boulevard Photographic. The clients, the ads, and photographs shown in this chapter, only begin to illustrate the breadth, but not the depth, of Boulevard's work. In the course of their careers, which began in the 1950s and ended in the 1990s, Northmore and McGuire's assignments would number not in the hundreds, but in the thousands. That McGuire, Northmore, and Boulevard Photographic came to so dominate the field of automotive advertising had much to do with personalities and timing, but mostly it hinged on the art and magic they invariably produced.

BLESS DE SOTO
for making seats that let you step out like a lady!

The smart way to go places...DE SOTO

CARS GONE BY

Boulevard had the dubious distinction of shooting the last ad for a number of makes. Soon after they shot this ad, DeSoto was gone. They also shot the last ads for Studebaker, Hudson, and Edsel.

SOLE SURVIVOR

Conceived in secret by a team of designers and engineers working in a rented house in Palm Springs, California, it was fitting that the introductory photography for the 1963 Studebaker Avanti would also be shot in the environs of Palm Springs. At the time, however, it was no secret that Studebaker was in trouble. Its demise would come in 1966. The Avanti, however, would survive as the product of Avanti Motor Corporation.

RELATED PRODUCTS

Not all of Boulevard's clients were in the business of selling cars. With an interest in making cars shine, Vista Car Wax was a long-time Boulevard client, as was Champion Spark Plugs. In fact, this Champion ad, which was shot in the studio and included a Jeep borrowed from the nearby "Boulevard" service station, was one of McGuire and Northmore's earliest assignments.

DON'T BE PUSHED AROUND **THIS** WINTER!

Your car will start fast with patented
FIVE-RIB CHAMPION SPARK PLUGS!

One side, '58 Corvette, cleaned *and* waxed

VISTA TIME: 18 minutes
DURATION: up to 6 months

Simoniz makes it as only Simoniz can—VISTA, for tough <u>real</u> paste wax beauty and protection. VISTA is <u>real</u> paste wax with cleaner in it—*turbo-whipped* so it spreads smoothly, dries and wipes off quickly. One easy application cleans, shines and protects your car for months... *try it.*

THREE DECADES OF MUSTANGS

From the beginning, Ford's Mustang has been an evolving breed. Over the years, Boulevard Photographic kept pace and helped establish and maintain the Mustang as an American icon.

OTHER PURSUITS

Northmore's interest in things mechanical led to a mutually profitable association with Mickey Rupp. Boulevard shot advertising materials for Rupp's mini-bikes and snowmobiles, while Rupp lent his engineering talents to some of Northmore's photographic inventions.

EXPANDING HORIZONS

Under the direction of Andy Nelson, Ford art directors commissioned experimental photography that stretched the imagination. In this case, a West Coast quarry provided a surreal background for Fords of unrealistic proportions.

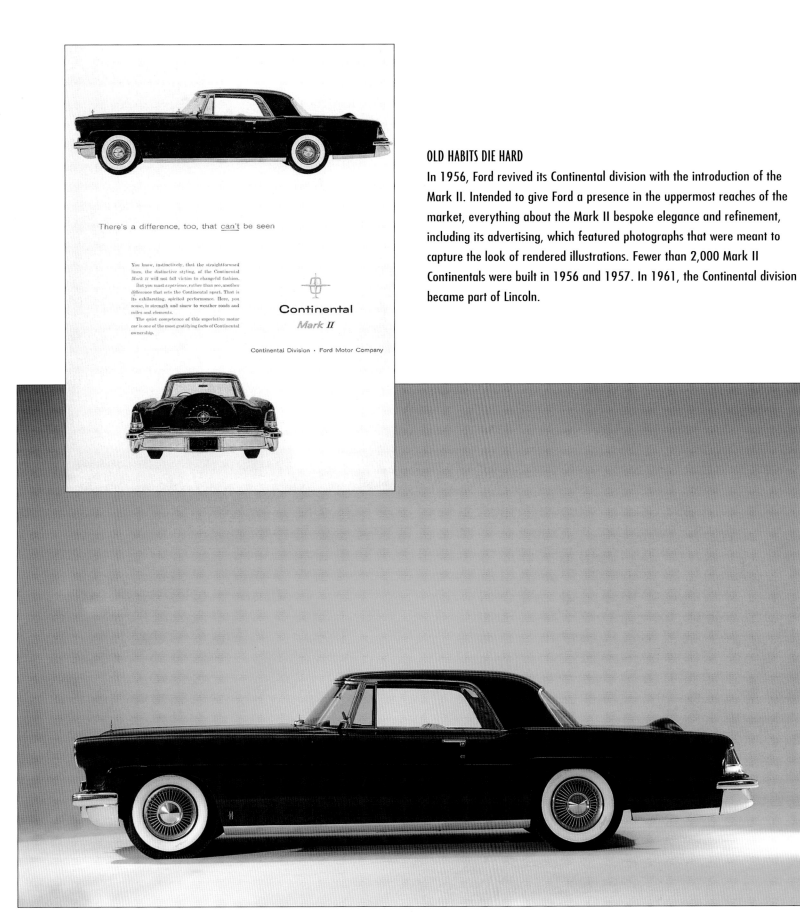

There's a difference, too, that can't be seen

You know, instinctively, that the straightforward lines, the distinctive styling, of the Continental *Mark II* will not fall victim to changeful fashion.

But you must *experience*, rather than see, another difference that sets the Continental apart. That is its exhilarating, spirited performance. Here, you sense, is strength and sinew to weather roads and miles and elements.

The quiet competence of this superlative motor car is one of the most gratifying facts of Continental ownership.

Continental
Mark II

Continental Division · Ford Motor Company

OLD HABITS DIE HARD

In 1956, Ford revived its Continental division with the introduction of the Mark II. Intended to give Ford a presence in the uppermost reaches of the market, everything about the Mark II bespoke elegance and refinement, including its advertising, which featured photographs that were meant to capture the look of rendered illustrations. Fewer than 2,000 Mark II Continentals were built in 1956 and 1957. In 1961, the Continental division became part of Lincoln.

Mercury's got it.
European elegance with an American Cougar wrapped around it.

WILD ANIMALS

During the 1960s, the art directors at Kenyon & Eckhardt on the Lincoln-Mercury account fell in love with using animals in its ads for the Comet and the Cougar. Though the public found these furry creatures charming, they were extremely difficult models to work with. Boo the dog would never sit still, and Chauncey the cat would only perform when plied with raw chicken necks.

DREAM MACHINES

While photography is an important tool for selling cars to the public, carmakers also use it to sell themselves on products and ideas. For example, in 1960, Plymouth stylists dreamed up the XNR as a spartan sports car, but then wondered how the concept would play in a more luxurious environment. Before going back to the drawing board, Boulevard was called upon to give the XNR a fantasy treatment.

DATSUN 280-ZX. THE MYSTIQUE GOES ON.

280-ZX Grand Luxury 2-seater with optional T-bar roof and gold accent

BROCHURES, BROCHURES, BROCHURES. . . .

Sales brochures and catalogs always accounted for the lion's share of Boulevard's work. This is because the shots needed to fill a single catalog could easily surpass the number of pictures a manufacturer was likely to use in a whole year's worth of advertising.

CAFE CONTINENTAL

Mandated by the Energy Policy and Conservation Act of 1975, CAFE standards forced major changes to automobiles and, consequently, advertising. By 1984, cars like the Lincoln Continental had become mere shadows of their former selves, and the images created by Boulevard would focus on efficiency rather than excess.

OH, WHAT A FEELING!

Successful importers such as Toyota relied upon Boulevard Photographic to make their products look "at home" in America. Cressida and Tercel may be foreign sounding names, but the images created by Boulevard were distinctly American.

MGB presents the world's biggest sunroof.

CLASSIC CARS. CLASSIC IMAGES.

Nothing represented British tradition better than the work of Art Director Marce Mayhew and the photography he commissioned from Northmore and McGuire for clients such as MG and Jaguar.

ART And MAGIC 4

WHEN Jimmy Northmore and Mickey McGuire began taking pictures, photography was seen mostly as a means to record images. And although there were those who considered the taking of pictures an art, the creation of images that were more than mere records was still considered the province of artists. With brushes and pens, artists could render virtually anything that could be imagined. They could make a car longer, lower, wider. They could put a car in any location. They could use light and form to present any mood. And, they could put a car in motion.

WIDE ANGLE "PULLED"
A view camera allows the photographer to tilt and swing the position of the film. When used in combination with a wide angle lens dramatic effects are possible.

Given the fact that McGuire and Northmore would shoot literally thousands of cars and trucks over their careers, one might assume that they were automotive enthusiasts and that this would have been one of the keys to their success. However, even though they clearly had a remarkable affinity for automotive subjects, neither started out nor ever became a real car nut. If they had, they might not have been able to approach a lowly Nash Rambler with the same enthusiasm as a lofty Lincoln Continental. And even though their work would inspire many advertising ideas, they also remained above the fray when it came to the intricacies of how one or another vehicle should or shouldn't be advertised. As they saw it, their job was to make every car and client look good, which they did time after time because they were the masters of the processes and possibilities of photography.

The View Camera

As with all photographers, the basic tool for McGuire and Northmore was the camera and their medium was film. Following the lead of George Eastman whose ads of over 100 years ago read, "You press the button, we do the rest," the photographic industry would continually strive to make picture-taking simpler and easier. In the decades after World War II, such efforts would be highlighted by the development of single lens reflex (SLR) cameras designed to utilize 35mm and 2-1/4-inch-square (6x6cm) roll films.

Boasting compactness, convenience, and ever more advanced and automated features and accessories, SLRs would become the tools of choice for many amateur and professional photographers alike. State-of-the-art SLRs would of course find their way into Boulevard Photographic's arsenal, but for the vast majority of their work, McGuire and Northmore would always rely on an ancient, hulking monster known as the 8x10 view camera. In fact, the one used by McGuire throughout his career was a prewar Ansco constructed largely of wood.

All eyes are on the "Rocket"! All eyes are on the most exciting motor car on the highway! It's Oldsmobile's sensational "88"—lowest-priced car with the "Rocket" Engine and Oldsmobile Hydra-Matic*. Try that "Rocket Ride" yourself!

OLDSMOBILE

THE "ROCKET" HYDRA-MATIC CAR !

Courtesy of the Engle Collection with permission of the Oldsmobile History Center

Whereas an SLR camera has a viewing system and film transport mechanism contained in a body onto which various lenses are attached, the essential components of a view camera are a lens panel, a bellows, and a back panel, which holds a focusing screen that is replaced by a film holder when an exposure is to be made. Focusing is controlled by adjusting the distance between the lens and the focusing screen, both of which slide fore and aft on rails. The lens and rear panels can also be made to slide or shift horizontally, rise or fall vertically, and swing or tilt around their central axis. Thus, when compared to an SLR, in which the position of the film plane is fixed by the camera's body, the view camera gives the photographer far greater control over image composition, shape, and perspective. For example, by moving the view camera's front or back panel up, down, or sideways, portions of the image can be excluded without having to move the camera. Swinging, pulling, or tilting the rear panel relative to the lens panel can be used to correct or distort the perspective of the image. However, even though McGuire and Northmore would use the view camera's full range of movements to great effect, the biggest reason for using a view camera was image size.

In terms of area, an 8x10 original is more than 16 times larger than one that measures 2 1/4x2 1/4—some 66 times bigger than the typical 35mm frame. A larger original obviously requires a lesser degree of enlargement in the process of reproduction, which translates to less loss of sharpness due to magnification. This was particularly important in the early days of color when films were extremely "grainy." As finer grain color films were developed, loss of image quality due to enlargement became less of a factor. Nevertheless, Northmore and McGuire would continue shooting 8x10 originals simply because that's what most clients preferred—they liked being able look at an transparency without having to squint through a magnifying lens.

SUPER "88" HOLIDAY COUPÉ. A GENERAL MOTORS VALUE.

Excitement rides with you . . . *when you ride a "Rocket"*
Oldsmobile! For here is a car more active than
your imagination . . . free and fleet and vibrantly alive in
every wonderful way! For taking off or taking a curve,
for smooth stopping and easy steering, for easing through
traffic or breezing along—you'll find that Oldsmobile
is different . . . *dramatically different!* And the brilliant beauty
is something you can't miss . . . up close or 'way
down the road. That's Oldsmobile's exclusive "flying color"
flair . . . the "Go-Ahead" look that matches the
"Rocket's" go-ahead spirit! See your dealer for a
demonstration. Get out of the ordinary . . . get into an OLDS!

Express yourself . . .
with *Flying Colors!*

OLDSMOBILE

MAKE A DATE WITH AN 88

In 1950, the state of the art in automotive advertising was rendered artwork. This Oldsmobile 88 ad (facing page) reflected the style of the time—carefully rendered sheet metal, white chrome, slightly exaggerated proportions, and more than a hint of speed. Five years later, the basic style had not changed dramatically, but the 1955 Olds 88 ad now featured photography. Clearly, photography was initially influenced by the look that advertisers had come to expect from artwork. And before photography would emerge as a distinct medium, photographers first had to prove that they could do everything that artists could.

SHOOTING A CAR LIKE A PIECE OF SILVER
One of the original photographs made by Northmore inside the tent he constructed on the stage of the old Detroit Music Hall.

TENTS AND FLYING FLATS

When it came to selling the automobile industry on the viability of photography, one of the biggest deterrents was controlling reflections. Photographers found that when taking a picture of an automobile outside against a beautiful background, the car became a gigantic mirror of sky, grass, and other extraneous reflections. And what with the importance of chrome as a key styling and selling feature in the immediate postwar years, the first challenge for automobile photographers was to produce clean "white chrome."

One of the most important breakthroughs or advancements that helped make photography a legitimate alternative to illustration occurred in 1949 when Northmore created his muslin tent on the old Detroit Music Hall stage. At the urging of Art Greenwald, Northmore took the same principles employed in tabletop photography, scaled them up about 2,000 percent and proved that he could render a large metallic object—in this case, a car—as beautifully as a piece of silver.

The tent was illuminated by batteries of trough lights, shone through from outside the tent to create diffused overall light. A hole just large

NATURAL TENT LIGHTING
A foggy day provides soft, diffuse lighting, eliminating unwanted reflections. As this shot taken in the foggy Bay Area shows, it can also make for a pretty dull picture.

enough for a camera lens was cut through one side. And *voila*, pure white chrome. Everyone loved the results and it didn't take long for clients and other photographers to jump on the tent studio bandwagon.

As good as tent lighting was, however, it was a cumbersome process and all the "tented" car pictures tended to look alike because of the uniformity of highlights and reflections. What was needed was some way to not only eliminate unwanted highlights and reflections, but to create interesting ones. And just when everybody else was constructing their tent studios, Boulevard raised the ante by employing the overhead or "flying" flat.

A flying flat was a rectangular, movable, car-sized reflective surface. Unlike the tent, which provided overall uniform lighting, the flying flat could be moved to alter the position or angle of highlights. Reflections could also be manipulated by the strategic placement of elements that would selectively absorb or reflect light. A white card or "wild flat" could reflect light to add a highlight to a fender or wheel. A dark cloth laid on the floor, or held to the side, could accentuate shape or add contrast.

The success of the flying flat led to the use of the "flying box" which combined the best attributes of tent lighting and movable flats. The flying box was essentially a flat that carried its own illumination. It was massive, heavy, and expensive, but it was a very creative and huge time-saving tool.

THE FLYING FLAT
Unlike the tent, the overhead or "flying" flat was movable and thus gave Northmore and McGuire a high degree of control over light and reflections.

75

LONGER. LOWER. WIDER.

The ability to render chrome photographically was a huge step, but illustrators still had one big advantage over photographers: They could make up for the aesthetic deficiencies of an automobile. In the early 1950s, the public wanted ever-bigger, more impressive, and imposing vehicles. And for all the advantages photography might have offered in terms of credibility, manufacturers were faced with the dilemma of what was more important: the reality of a photograph or presenting an automobile in a fashion that accentuated—or exaggerated—its best attributes.

When Northmore was shooting scrap for the artists at New Center Studio to help them with their illustrations, he had figured out ways to alter the proportions of a vehicle as he was enlarging

BIG AS A HOUSE
With their curved-back film holders, McGuire and Northmore could add inches or feet to the length of a car (some of which, like this Lincoln, already looked miles long). They knew they'd reached the limit when the car's wheels ceased being round.

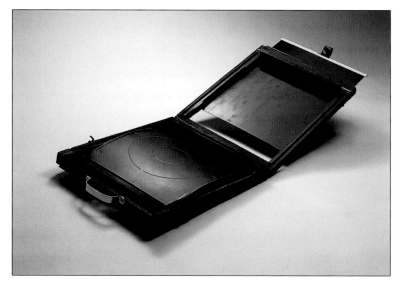

BOULEVARD'S SECRET WEAPON
One of the original curved-back film holders that gave McGuire and Northmore the unique ability to stretch cars in their photographs. It was simple, but effective. Not shown in this picture are the fake knobs that were added to the view finder to make clients think the device was more complicated than it actually was.

black-and-white prints. By tilting the paper under the enlarger, he could stretch the car in one direction or the other. He also noted that by bending the paper, he could elongate an image along one axis. This was great for the purpose of artist's scrap. It occurred to Jimmy that there ought to be a way to do this with the camera.

The answer was Boulevard's curved film holder—an ingeniously simple device which Northmore actually credits to McGuire. By curving the film, they knew they could produce an elongated image on a transparency. The only complication was that in order to see how it was going to elongate, they had to have a ground-glass finder that precisely matched the same curve as the film holder. So they recruited studio technician Bob Schmidt to fabricate a half-dozen film holders that were about an inch thick, with a curved base so that the film could be held in an arch. He then made a holder with an identically curved piece of frosted plastic to act as a ground-glass finder. The amount of elongation or stretch they were able to achieve was a matter of the image size. Maximum stretch was achieved when the car took up about 8 inches of the film's 10-inch horizontal dimension. Moving the camera further away from the subject—making the car take up only the

center 6 inches of the film—would obviously yield less stretch. The biggest things McGuire and Northmore had to worry about were an uneven stretch, which would occur if the car wasn't centered, or ending up with a car that was bent like a banana as a result of straying too far from right angles in setting up the camera relative to the car. Of course, if they stretched a car too far, they also ran the danger of producing wheels and tires that appeared to be elliptical instead of round.

These stretch film holders were both effective and ingeniously simple, but it took a long time for anybody to figure out what McGuire and Northmore were doing. To add to the mystery, they installed bogus knobs on the outside of the finder to give clients and onlookers the impression that they were using some mechanical device to control and adjust the elongation.

Initially, those clients most interested in stretching cars were those with the biggest cars, such as Lincoln. But eventually, McGuire

BANANA BOAT
An early test using Boulevard's curved-back film holders. It shows how the process could bend the image of a car if everything wasn't lined up perfectly.

ART AND INSPIRATION

By 1960, McGuire and Northmore had developed the means to make photography do many things. However, rendering all of the inspirational design elements of Cadillac's 1961 models—graceful silhouette, increased headroom, delicately-formed roof lines, uninterrupted panoramic vision—were still beyond the scope of photography.

and Northmore would put the stretch on just about everything—even Ramblers.

McGuire and Northmore successfully employed their secret stretch film holders for a number of years, but eventually found an even better way of achieving the same results—the anamorphotic lens. Such lenses incorporated an optical system that used prisms to alter the scale of images both vertically and horizontally. Interestingly, the idea wasn't new. Prisms had been used to correct or distort images since the late 1800s, but it was the introduction of wide-screen movies in the 1950s that spurred the development of the lenses employed by McGuire and Northmore.

Although the public loved the panoramic proportions of wide-screen movies, they presented a real problem for theater owners. Cinemascope, VistaVision, and other formats were all slightly different in their panoramic effect. Anamorphotic lenses were developed for use on theater projectors to accommodate the different formats, which otherwise would have required their own lenses. McGuire and Northmore reasoned that if an anamorphotic lens could adjust the vertical and horizontal scales of projected images, it could just as easily be applied to images in a camera. Boulevard photographers were now able to exaggerate the long, low look of automobiles with increased speed and ease.

In addition to the anamorphotic lens, they used wide-angle lenses to great effect until fuel-efficiency concerns changed consumer tastes and made it less fashionable to stretch cars. In fact, it became as common to use a telephoto lens to foreshorten vehicles.

CONTROLLED STRETCH

A young Northmore, with art director John Dignan, shown using an anamorphotic lens, which offered greater control and flexibility than Boulevard's original curved-back film holders.

IMPOSING POWER
The wide-angle lens was used to exaggerate other attributes and proportions. In this shot, there's no question that the emphasis is the 428 Cobra Jet power that's under this Cougar's mile-wide hood.

PRETOUCHING VERSUS RETOUCHING

McGuire was not just known for being tall, but for always thinking about pictures—especially on the road. One day in the early 1950s, while driving into the sun, McGuire found himself adjusting his seating position relative to the windshield tinted band. This not only made it easier to see, but it made the view more attractive. He found that the darkened sky, contrasted with the brightly lit highway, drew attention to the cars on the road and made the scene more interesting. He reasoned that he could use partial or variegated filters to add interest to his pictures. Although such filters put in front of the lens would be something that many automotive photographers would ultimately use, McGuire and Northmore were among the first.

According to McGuire: "When you see something in a picture that reflects light that is brighter than its source, your mind tells you that something has been done. However, if this unnatural effect is obvious, then the photographer has failed." McGuire perfected the use of four basic types of filters that, individually and collectively, were used to remarkable effect. The first involved the use of neutral-density materials to adjust the intensity of light with no effect on color. The second used colored filters to correct or adjust the temperature of the light from cool to warm. He also used strongly colored gels or filters to totally change the overall color of the light. And finally, polarizing filters were used to eliminate or shift reflections.

Polarizing filters incorporate a rotating filter or screen that will transmit light only along a particular plane. Thus, it makes it possible to hold back light rays that are reflected from one direction or another. By

LIKE LOOKING THROUGH A TINTED WINDSHIELD
Same time, same spot, same Ford Thunderbird, different picture. A side-by-side comparison of how selectively filtering light can add emphasis and interest to a picture.

UNDER TOTAL CONTROL

Neutral-density gels reduce the intensity of the sun, while a polarizing filter places highlights on the roof and hood of this Ford Thunderbird. A color correcting filter gives this dry lake bed a warm glow.

COOL VERSUS WARM

In this case, the image that Ford was seeking wasn't warm and fuzzy. Although this picture employs neutral-density and polarizing filters, only a minimal amount of correction has been applied to alter light temperature, so the image remains cool.

rotating the filter, it is possible to remove a reflection from a windshield while highlighting a reflection along the hood. While some photographers consider the use of "polo screens" and other filtering techniques to be artifice, McGuire and Northmore considered it all part of their job in creating ideal photographic images. It's what McGuire would call "pre-touching rather than retouching," which often made the difference between a mundane photograph or a thing of beauty.

The creation of an ideal picture for McGuire or Northmore began as it would for most photographers: selecting the ideal location,

COLOR ALTERATION

Sometimes, filtering goes beyond mere temperature correction. This picture was shot through a strong yellow gel to give the scene an exaggerated autumn glow.

composing the subject and background, and making appropriate calculations for shutter speed and f-stop. Only after performing all the steps that normally go into making a photograph as God and Eastman Kodak would see it, would Boulevard photographers deign to apply their own controls. Historically, photographers had paid more attention to the intensity than the temperature of light. But McGuire believed that pictures, like people, have personalities, and that people respond more positively to warmth than to coolness. That's why he and Northmore were among the first to try to confine shooting their location pictures to the golden light of a sunrise or sunset. When they were unable to do so, they invariably would employ temperature-correcting filters to try to shoot for that kind of glow.

Producing variations in light intensity might require several separate layers of gels. Constant fiddling and adjustment of each successive layer were necessary to produce soft edges and subtle gradations, otherwise an observer might be tipped off that something unnatural had been done. Once the overall mood and effect were set, they could use the polarizing filter to reduce or enhance reflections. And if a particular reflection needed to be softened or accentuated, out would come the jar of Vaseline that McGuire claims put his four kids through college.

People have attributed McGuire's mastery over camera controls to his physical size. The fact that he is seven feet tall allowed him to actually reach around to the filter holder in front of the lens to make these adjustments himself, all the while keeping an eye on what was happening in the ground glass. Physical dexterity aside, McGuire always had an innate sense for artistry with light. In fact, the quality of light was so important to McGuire that he took up residence in Palm Springs, California, primarily because of the naturally ideal light.

MOTION

Portraying motion is one of the most difficult challenges a still photographer faces.

For the purposes of automobile advertising, the photographer's assignment is invariably to capture the sensation of speed while keeping the car sharply in focus. This normally means moving the camera at the same rate of speed as the subject, while relying on shutter speed to record a blur that shows the speed differential between the subject and background.

This can be accomplished by "panning" the camera with the car as it moves. But as simple as this sounds, it's an exercise fraught with variables, not the least of which is the coordination of the camera operator. These problems can be overcome by shooting from another vehicle moving at the same speed as the subject. However, as the vehicles drive along together, the background and lighting are subject to change. Plus, the acrobatics involved in car-to-car shooting makes the use of a large-format camera impractical. It's an endeavor best left to motor-driven 35-millimeter cameras.

EARLY MOTION

Capturing motion with a large-format camera was considered difficult, if not impossible. Using sensors to activate the camera shutter, Boulevard proved it could be done, but it was still no easy feat.

Early on, Northmore and McGuire came up with a device that facilitated the making of "pan shots" with a large-format camera. It employed an electronic solenoid that would activate the camera's shutter as the moving vehicle tripped a sensor on the road surface. This meant all the photographer had to do was to match the motion of the camera with the car's, which was still no mean feat. But the device served well until Northmore came up with an even better solution.

In 1983, Northmore created and patented what he would call the "Synchronized Motion Rig," an ingenious device that transferred the vehicle's motion directly to the camera. Although it sounds complicated, its workings were fairly simple. Using an electric winch, the car was pulled via a lightweight cable, which was nearly invisible to the camera. On the other end of the car was another cable, which was attached to a stationary hydraulic cylinder. A second "slave" cylinder was attached to the camera which was mounted in a dolly that moved on precision rails. Pulling the car forced hydraulic fluid out the first cylinder and out through a 50- to 100-foot hydraulic line to the "slave" cylinder, which would move the camera and dolly at precisely the same speed and over the same distance as the car. Once the car and camera were moving together, all the photographer had to do was open the shutter. The longer it stayed open, the more blurred the effect. It wasn't necessary to move the car far or fast. As a rule, Northmore found that moving the car 4 feet through the course of a 4-second exposure was more than enough to simulate a car traveling 60 miles per hour.

Northmore built two rigs. The first version employed cables instead of hydraulic lines to transfer the movement from car to camera. It worked well but took a long time to set up and was not easily portable. The second rig was engineered with the assistance of Northmore's long-time friend and mechanical-engineering genius, Mickey Rupp. This rig not only added hydraulics, it was quick and easy to set up, and the whole thing could be packed away and transported in one box. Both versions served Boulevard's photographers and many clients well. As an interesting side note, at the same time Northmore was developing his rig, George Ealovega, one of his former assistants then living in England, came up with a device that did essentially the same thing. The difference was that Ealovega's rig relied on sophisticated electronic controls and cost about $70,000, whereas Northmore figures his cost only about $5,000.

The Synchronized Motion Rig allowed Boulevard's photographers to capture real motion with precision control and repeatability. It also provided extraordinary flexibility. Coupled with a slow shutter speed, the vehicle only had to move a few feet in the process of creating a motion picture. So the rig worked equally well in the studio or on location. It also gave Boulevard photographers the ability to put any vehi-

RIG SETUP
Before Northmore came up with a hydraulic system to transfer the movement of the car to the dolly-mounted camera, his motion rig relied on cables and pulleys.

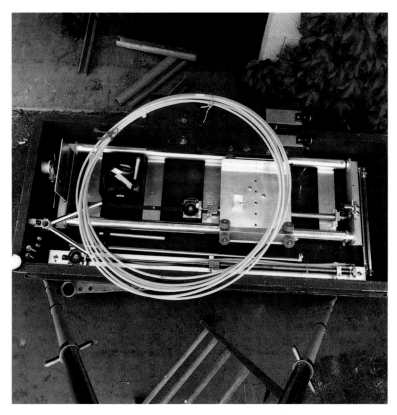

MOTION TO GO
With the assistance of Mickey Rupp, the motion rig was re-engineered. The improved version was not only quicker and easier to set up, it was designed so the whole thing could fit in a box for easy transport.

AT REST AND IN MOTION

A Chevrolet Celebrity parked in a studio setting, perfectly lit and in front of a cityscape painting complete with twinkling lights. With the motion rig engaged, in the span of four seconds and four feet, the wheels are turning, the background is moving, and the car appears to be traveling at highway speed while remaining in perfect focus.

A DIFFERENT SENSE OF MOTION
Though not fluid or particularly realistic, multiple exposure techniques, as used with this 427 Corvette, can be dramatic.

cle in motion—even styling prototype cars without engines. And, any format camera could be used.

Before and after the motion rig, Boulevard used a number of other "tricks" to create the illusion of motion. One was based on a simple multiple exposure technique. They would take a picture of the car, turn off all the lights in the studio, turn on the lights of the car, then make a second exposure while the car was backing up. Or, instead of moving the car, they'd move the camera. In either case, the illusion of motion was created by the use of a light source (head or taillight) on the subject.

They also found ways to simulate motion without moving the car or the camera. One way was to use the set painter's art to create the illusion of movement. Other tricks involved brushing or blowing various powdery substances. But among the most clever tricks was one that involved no motion on the part of the car, the camera, or the background.

Anyone who has ever looked through smudged eyeglasses or a greasy fingerprint is familiar with a blurred image. What causes the blurriness is refraction, which results from a change in the direction of a ray of light passing from one transparent medium into another of a different density. Since glass is one medium and grease is another, you end up with a blur.

Cinematographers have long used grease or petroleum jellies to produce soft-focus images or to create the attitude of soft, romantic vignettes. McGuire and Northmore became proficient at controlling

TELLTALE TAILLIGHTS
By using a light source—in this case the taillights—and multiple exposures, this 1967 Dodge Coronet was set in "motion."

refraction to create the illusion of motion. They found that smudging or striating the grease in one direction produced a blur or a refraction in the opposite direction. Thus, by selectively applying grease to a piece of glass in front of the camera lens, they could blur portions of the image. In the case of cars, creating a blur on a wheel, headlight, or the background could give you the appearance of motion. Of course, the trick was to create the blur in the proper direction.

PAINTED MOTION

Before the motion rig, the illusion of speed was often left to the set painter. To illustrate the "fleetness" of the 1963 Mercury Meteor, an elaborately painted floor and studio back wall were created.

GREASE JOBS

Neither the Mustang nor the Corvette in either of these pictures is moving. In fact, absolutely nothing is in motion in either picture. All the movement is phony and achieved by the selective application of grease on a glass in front of the lens. This radically customized Sting Ray was not a "factory" job. The car and photo were commissioned by a Detroit radio station as a "drive-time" promotion.

OTHER TRICKS AND TREATS

Beyond techniques of lighting, controls, special lenses, and motion, the photographers at Boulevard had a magic hat that they would, on occasion, reach into for other unique effects. Some of these were fairly crude in their level of sophistication, but others required an unbelievable amount of preparation or materials to "work the magic." Clients loved the inventiveness they found at Boulevard and were constantly challenging the photographers with new ideas that had never been done before. One thing was certain—no matter what kind of wacky or complicated idea an art director might come up with, Boulevard was only too happy to oblige.

Whether it was using their front-screen projection system to broaden the availability of background possibilities, perfecting cutaway or see-through techniques, adding visual interest with reflective surfaces, or giving mother nature a run for her money by creating any number of environmental conditions inside the studio, McGuire and Northmore truly became masters of illusion.

FRONT PROJECTION

Before the advent of computer graphics and blue-screen matting, cinematographers used front projection as a way to put actors in front of backgrounds that weren't really there. Rear projection systems came first. As the name implies, background images were projected onto the back of translucent screen positioned behind the subject. Such systems took up a lot of space and the results weren't too convincing. In a front-screen projection setup, the background image is projected from a source located with the camera, in front of the subject, and onto a special screen behind the subject. The background image doesn't show up on the subject because the image that comes from the projector is invisible to anything but the screen. Front projection setups were expensive and extremely rare in still photography studios. But in the interest of offering full service and maximum creative flexibility, Boulevard not only had its own, but had the biggest screen available.

HOLLYWOOD MAGIC

In the wintry scene created for a Rupp snowmobile ad, Boulevard's front projection system was used to create a realistic setting. It could also introduce purely abstract backgrounds, as with the 1968 Ford Torino, which also exhibits the stretching effect of an anamorphotic lens.

MULTIPLE EXPOSURES

Multiple-exposure techniques were used to show things that were normally hidden from the eye—things like chassis and mechanical components or seating and cargo capacity. A cutaway or ghost image produced by multiple exposures involved a number of steps. The number of exposures, of course, was determined by the number of things that needed to be shown. For instance, if you wanted to show the car's engine and chassis through its exterior sheet metal, two exposures would be necessary. The process seems straightforward and simple but requires strict attention to registration and the lighting of the individual exposures.

X-RAY PHOTOS

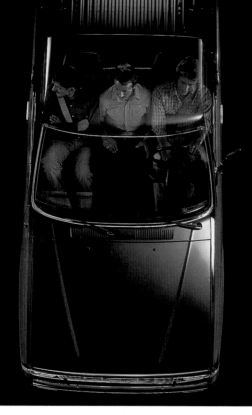

STEP 1

To illustrate the three-across seating in a Toyota pickup truck, the cab of the truck is first photographed in the studio against a black background. The lighting is arranged so that the roof over the passenger area is black or unexposed. Multiple exposures, covering variations in lighting and aperture would be made.

STEP 2

One of the previous exposures is developed to create a guide for a second setup, in which the passengers are outside of the truck but positioned exactly as they would be if they were sitting in the truck. Lighting and aperture are controlled so that everything but the passengers is black or unexposed. The undeveloped shots from the first setup are exposed again.

STEP 3

When the film is finally developed, the passengers now appear to be in the truck. Areas of the film that were unexposed or underexposed in one setup, such as the roof, appear to fade away.

STUDIO EFFECTS

Before the advent of computer graphics and blue-screen matting, cinematographers used front projection as a way to put actors in front of backgrounds that weren't really there. Rear projection systems came first. As the name implies, background images were projected onto the back of translucent screen positioned behind the subject. Such systems took up a lot of space and the results weren't too convincing. In a front-screen projection setup, the background image is projected from a source located with the camera, in front of the subject, and onto a special screen behind the subject. The background image doesn't show up on the subject because the image that comes from the projector is invisible to anything but the screen. Front projection setups were expensive and extremely rare in still photography studios. But in the interest in offering full service and maximum creative flexibility, Boulevard not only had its own, but had the biggest screen available.

WHEN DAY BECOMES NIGHT

What would otherwise be a standard studio shot takes on an air of mystery thanks to a wet floor and dry-ice fog swirling around this Toyota. Similarly, fog is used to diffuse and carry the glow of lights behind the columns to silhouette the foreground Toyota wagons. Amazingly, the Toyota trio in the second shot was actually photographed in full daylight. The whole scene was underexposed and then re-exposed again using bright strobe lights to illuminate the fog.

TINY MIRROR

The single star-like highlight on the nose of this Nissan 300 ZX was produced by a tiny reflective jewel glued to the emblem. Grease applied to the glass in front of the lens created streaks of light.

STUDIO STORM

A rainy night, created in the studio with umbrellas and a mirror placed under the camera lens to reflect the Thunderbird's imposing chrome grille.

5 SHOOTER'S GALLERY

IN the course of their careers, Jimmy Northmore and Mickey McGuire shot literally thousands of pictures. That they remained at the top of their game for so long can be attributed to a number of reasons, not the least of which was believing in the old film actor's adage that "you're only as good as your last picture."

Indeed, in a business as competitive and as ever-changing as advertising, you can't afford to rest on your laurels. This helps explain why Northmore and McGuire continually strove to find ways to make better pictures—always honing their own talents and abilities, developing new techniques and equipment, and doing whatever it took to produce images that would meet and exceed the expectations of their clients.

The body of work that resulted is impressive not just for its size, but for its legacy to the fields of photography and automotive advertising. These pictures shaped how generations of people came to view and feel about automobiles. And while all of the pictures were individually and collectively important to the business of Boulevard Photographic, it should come as no surprise that Northmore and McGuire find certain ones more or less memorable and significant.

This Shooter's Gallery is a collection of pictures that Jimmy Northmore and Mickey McGuire singled out as their best or most memorable work.

EKTACHROME TRANSPARENCY BY JIMMY NORTHMORE, 1965.

JIMMY NORTHMORE
Magician and Artist

> *"What we have in this photograph is a
> picture of a car going
> 60 miles per hour in
> the studio under total control."*
> —Jimmy Northmore

SUBJECT: DODGE CHARGER
LOCATION: BOULEVARD STUDIO
CAMERA/FILM: 8X10 VIEW CAMERA/EKTACHROME TRANSPARENCY
ART DIRECTOR: JIM HANNA

There were times when a client had a very clear idea of what they wanted to see in a picture. Most times, however, we'd find ourselves working with agency art directors to figure out how best to visualize a theme or idea. Clients were known to come up with headlines and advertising themes that weren't easy to visualize. That's why I really relished the times when you had a concept where the words and pictures went together. In this case, the art director gave me "the night belongs to Charger" and said, "see what you can do with it." Some might have entertained the notion of going out into the night to shoot, but I started by going to my files and pulling a 35-millimeter slide for a background. Using it as a guide for light, color, and perspective, I created a rainy night in the studio. I covered the floor with a shiny plastic sheet to produce a foreground area of reflections for the ad's headline and copy. To soften the reflections and to add a sense of motion, I selectively applied grease to the glass in front of the lens and three small strips of green gel to bring the color of the background into the foreground. After making the studio shot, I added the background to the undeveloped film through masking and double exposure.

SUBJECT: LINCOLN CONTINENTAL
LOCATION: OUTDOOR
CAMERA/FILM: 8X10 VIEW CAMERA/EKTACHROME TRANSPARENCIES
ART DIRECTOR: DAVE MILLER

I've loved airplanes all of my life, so I was always happy whenever they could be used to add interest or, as clients like to say, to help "position" a car in the minds of consumers. In this shot, which I set up at an airfield in Southern California, the planes added to the composition as well as its interest. The red cowls on the Sopwith and Nieuport and the red Fokker biplane model formed a triangle to help focus attention on the car. So even if you didn't care about airplanes, it was hard to miss the Continental. I was also an avid sailor. So I was almost as happy when a picture called for the use of boats.

SUBJECT: TRIUMPH TR-7
LOCATION: DAYTONA BEACH
CAMERA/FILM: 8X10 VIEW CAMERA/EKTACHROME TRANSPARENCY
ART DIRECTOR: MARCE MAYHEW

Over the years, we shot a lot of cars that, for one reason or another are no longer with us. This picture was made for the catalog that introduced the convertible version of Triumph's TR-7. I always found this car's sculptured body work interesting and a challenge to shoot. Unfortunately, such attributes didn't translate to sales. This picture appears as a sort wistful reminder of the TR-7 and all the other cars that came and went like the tides.

SUBJECT: 1976 LINCOLN CONTINENTAL
LOCATION: STUDIO
CAMERA/FILM: 8X10 VIEW CAMERA/EKTACHROME TRANSPARENCY
ART DIRECTOR: DAVE MILLER

The goal here was to give the client a theatrical lighting effect which required producing a hard, sharp shadow underneath the car. To achieve this effect, the lighting setup was somewhat unique. We hung the overhead flat to get the proper reflections, then used a huge spotlight to cast the shadow. The tricky part was getting the spotlight in there without destroying the lighting on the rest of the car. The "hard shadow" became a visual element that was used consistently throughout an entire campaign.

SUBJECT: PONTIAC GTO
LOCATION: BOULEVARD STUDIO
CAMERA/FILM: 8X10 VIEW CAMERA/EKTACHROME TRANSPARENCY
ART DIRECTOR: MARTY LIEBERMAN

The Pontiac GTO wasn't just the prototype "muscle car," it was also a classic example of "image building." The GTO was to become the "tiger," boasting feline attributes like paws where other cars had mere tires. This is an experimental photo I made, using a styling prototype for the 1966 model, to show how the tiger theme might be used to flatter GTO drivers as well as their cars.

SUBJECT: 1960 DODGE
LOCATION: CAPE COD
CAMERA/FILM: 8X10 VIEW CAMERA/EKTACHROME TRANSPARENCY
ART DIRECTOR: FRED PECK

Fred Peck was one of our earliest and best customers. In 1959, he hired both Mickey and I to take a crew to Cape Cod where we shot photos for all of the 1960 Dodge sales catalogs and advertising. With hundreds of pictures to shoot, we couldn't afford to wait around for the natural light to be ideal for every picture. So the use of what we call "controls" was absolutely critical. Here I used neutral-density gels, a polarizing filter, and cards to reflect light back into the rear chrome and details, to turn an extremely bright, back-lit situation into a pleasant sunset.

SUBJECT: 1974 DODGE
LOCATION: BOULEVARD STUDIO
CAMERA/FILM: 8X10 VIEW CAMERA/EKTACHROME
TRANSPARENCY
ART DIRECTOR: JIM HANNA

In addition to advertising, we did a huge amount of catalog work. As a result we were often called upon to illustrate mechanical features. Making such pictures attractive as well as informative was always a challenge. In this case, the client wanted to show various chassis and suspension components without going to the trouble and expense of making a cut-away. After some head scratching, it occurred to me that I might be able to use mirrors in much the same way that display makers sometimes employed them to give people a glimpse of the underside of things. Getting mirrors large and strong enough to drive a car on turned out to be somewhat of a problem. I ended up using a number of four-by-eight foot pieces that were made from a special and costly plastic. It also took a lot of time to paint and detail the underside of the car. And of course, it was no easy task to light and compose everything to eliminate unwanted reflections. But in the end, the client was delighted and so were the writers, whose copy was ultimately highlighted in colors to match the parts in the photo.

SUBJECT: BOULEVARD STUDIO PROMOTION
LOCATION: STUDIO
CAMERA/FILM: 8X10 VIEW CAMERA/EKTACHROME TRANSPARENCIES
ART DIRECTOR: JIMMY NORTHMORE

Ads typically don't include bylines crediting photographers, writers, or anyone else for their work. So we were obliged to promote the services of Boulevard Photographic ourselves. I created this shot for a promotional poster back when Flip Wilson's line "The devil made me do it" was popular. As the guy who was usually considered to be pretty serious and conservative, a lot of people were surprised, not just to see my name in place of the devil's, but that I'd be party to something so risqué. That of course was the whole idea—to let people know that Boulevard was full of surprises. However, even we were surprised by the popularity of this poster. We must have sent out over a thousand of these things. It was a huge hit with clients and went on to become a genuine collector's item with Excalibur owners and enthusiasts.

SUBJECT: NISSAN 300 ZX
LOCATION: STUDIO
CAMERA/FILM: 8X10 VIEW CAMERA/EKTACHROME TRANSPARENCIES
ART DIRECTOR: DAVE MILLER

The motion rig gave life to many ideas. When Nissan introduced a new generation of ZXs, the motion rig was used to give the model designations and the cars both an image of speed.

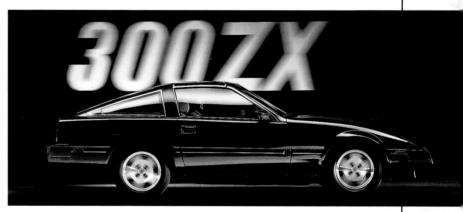

SUBJECT: 1984 CORVETTE
LOCATION: OUTDOOR
CAMERA/FILM: 8X10 VIEW CAMERA/EKTACHROME TRANSPARENCIES
ART DIRECTOR: GENE BUTERA

The introduction of the new-style Corvette in 1984 also marked the debut performance for my motion rig. The photo of the silver car was made in the parking lot of Rupp Marine in Stuart, Florida. We ended up there because Mickey Rupp, a long-time friend, client, and supporter of Boulevard Photographic, had applied his mechanical and engineering genius to the fabrication of the rig's components. The client was Gene Butera. Before going to work for Chevrolet's ad agency, he'd been the art director of *Car and Driver* magazine, so he had a pretty good idea of what real speed and motion ought to look like. And although he wanted to see the rig work, he was more than a little skeptical. However, after making a series of test shots, he was sold on the results and the creative possibilities of the rig. The shot of the silver car inspired the shot used in the center spread of the four-page introductory ad. The head-on shot of the red car was another rig shot, taken later in California. It became the cover. The success of these Corvette pictures opened the door to many more assignments. They also led to refinements in the design of my motion rig. Again with the help of Mickey Rupp, we built a second version that was quicker and easier to set up and a lot more portable. It employed hydraulics instead of cables to transfer the motion of the car to the camera, and the whole thing could be packed away and transported in one box.

SUBJECT: 1966 MERCURY
LOCATION: BOULEVARD STUDIO
CAMERA/FILM: 8X10 VIEW CAMERA/EKTACHROME TRANSPARENCIES
ART DIRECTOR: WALTER GRANBERG

In the mid-1960s, a "bigger is better" philosophy prevailed at Mercury. The objective was to make Mercurys look more like Lincolns and less like Fords. So for 1966, we pulled out all the stops. In these pictures I not only stretched the car's proportions to the limits of credibility, the setting implied that this Mercury might be at home inside a baronial mansion. Pulling off such ideas, which on the surface might seem far-fetched or even bizarre, tested the skills of not only the photographer, but also of our stylists. When it came to getting the props, models, costumes, and coordinating the sets, Boulevard's stylists were always among the best in the business.

SUBJECT: JAGUAR XJ6
LOCATION: OUTDOOR
CAMERA/FILM: 8X10 VIEW CAMERA/EKTACHROME TRANSPARENCY
ART DIRECTOR: MARCE MAYHEW

Mickey and I both had the good fortune to do a lot of work for Jaguar. This particular picture is memorable because of what happened seconds after I took it. This pastoral setting was on a real, working horse farm in Louisville, Kentucky. And I had just clicked the shutter for this picture when one of the grooms came running down the pathway from the barn, shouting that a horse was giving birth. Fortunately, it was the last shot of the day, so we left the camera and everything else right where it was and ran off down the path to witness the birth of another thoroughbred.

SUBJECT: 1976 JAGUAR XJS
LOCATION: BOULEVARD STUDIO
CAMERA/FILM: 8X10 VIEW CAMERA/EKTACHROME TRANSPARENCIES
ART DIRECTOR: MARCE MAYHEW

Jaguar advertising and sales literature usually stressed a sense of tradition that lent itself to location shooting. So it was rare that we'd find ourselves with a Jaguar in the studio. However, in 1976 the new XJS represented something of a break with tradition. Working with a new car and finding the lighting and angles that work best is always an interesting challenge. And although many people would always see the XJS as the less attractive successor to the E-type, when viewed in the right light, the XJS was clearly a car with a distinctive style and character.

SUBJECT: 1969 CADILLACS
LOCATION: OUTDOOR
CAMERA/FILM: 8X10 VIEW CAMERA/EKTACHROME TRANSPARENCY
ART DIRECTOR: BOB TOAY

This turned out to be a very expensive ad shoot, but not for obvious reasons. Getting a dozen Cadillacs out to the desert, cleaned up, set up, and photographed at various times of the day was a major undertaking, but the biggest problem occurred after we wrapped up the shoot. While moving the cars out of the desert, we were suddenly engulfed in a severe sandstorm. The effects weren't immediately obvious, but upon close inspection it was revealed that the blasting sand had pitted the windshields and dulled the chrome of all 12 cars. Since these cars had been acquired through dealers and were earmarked for future sale, every damaged piece had to be replaced. The result was an astronomical repair bill that our insurance company was none too happy to pay.

SUBJECT: 1965 CHRYSLER
LOCATION: BOULEVARD STUDIO
CAMERA/FILM: 8X10 VIEW CAMERA/EKTACHROME TRANSPARENCIES
ART DIRECTOR: ROY GETMAN

The art director behind these pictures was one who I'd previously not done a lot of work with, so I was somewhat surprised when he called with what amounted to a challenge: He wanted to see if I could make a color picture that was basically black, white, and gray. What he wanted to see had really nothing to do with illustrating anything in particular about the cars. What he was after was a unique "look"—a sort of visual mnemonic—that would at once distinguish and identify this campaign, which was something that artists were almost always striving for. Still, from a technical standpoint, this was an odd request. And fulfilling it forced me to employ some very unusual, high-contrast lighting, which produced a dramatic, almost surrealistic effect. The shot without the model is the original test I made to show that it could be done. The other is one in a series of pictures that employed this high-contrast lighting technique and was used in a campaign.

SUBJECT: 1967 DODGE
LOCATION: BOULEVARD STUDIO
CAMERA/FILM: 8X10 VIEW CAMERA/EKTACHROME TRANSPARENCY
ART DIRECTOR: JIM HANNA

The "Dodge Rebellion" was one of the best known and most enduring campaigns of the 1960s. And because it ran for so long, we were constantly challenged to find new or different ways of illustrating the rebellion theme. This was made easier by the fact that we could always rely on the "Dodge Girl" to add interest and help tell a story. One thing people may not have noticed was that there was more than one Dodge Girl. The campaign began with us shooting still photography with a model named Gerri Sands. And although she would always be the girl in catalogs and brochures, a different model was featured in TV commercials and ads. That Dodge ended up with two people for the same role was due in part to the kind of rivalries that sometimes existed between different departments in the same company.

SUBJECT: 1957 DODGE
LOCATION: SELFRIDGE AIR FORCE BASE
CAMERA/FILM: 8X10 VIEW CAMERA/EKTACHROME TRANSPARENCIES
ART DIRECTOR: FRED PECK

Just a year after I went to foggy San Francisco to get location pictures for Dodge with soft, diffuse lighting, the client wanted something different. Although the campaign and mood for 1957 still called for outdoor locations, the client now wanted pictures full of brightness and sparkle. This is an example of one such picture I made at the Selfridge Air Force Base just outside of Detroit. Technically, it's not one of my favorites, but it does feature two things I liked very much. One was an airplane. The other was the car. This red and white Lancer hardtop happened to belong to me. It was equipped with a "D-500" option package, which included a 245-horsepower "Hemi" engine. And I can attest to the performance of this early factory hot rod thanks to jousts with an identical twin that belonged to Fred Peck, the art director for the Dodge account and for this picture.

Step into the wonderful world of AUTODYNAMICS

It unleashes a hurricane of power!

When you slip behind the wheel of this Swept-Wing '57 Dodge, you step into a new world of road mastery. Autodynamics has unleashed the thundering power of a new aircraft-type V-8 engine, teamed it with new Push-Button TorqueFlite that packs a 1-2 punch. You sweep along in a low-slung beauty only 4½ feet high, cradled and cushioned by Torsion-Aire Ride that isolates engine vibration, noise and road shock. You have never seen, felt, owned anything like it.

It turns a tornado of torque
It breaks through the vibration barrier
It is swept-wing mastery of motion

SWEPT·WING '57 Dodge

SUBJECT: 1970 FORD MUSTANG
LOCATION: PALM SPRINGS, CALIFORNIA
CAMERA/FILM: 8X10 VIEW CAMERA/EKTACHROME TRANSPARENCIES
ART DIRECTOR: JOHN DIGNAN

These photographs were part of a light-hearted Ford campaign that aimed
to say that anyone with a Mustang was bound to get more than their fair
share of attention. It was an idea that lent itself to many interpretations. It
also called for all kinds of models. In the football scene, the part of the
referee, who is adored because of his shiny new Mustang, is played by
Mickey's long-time assistant, Wally Sternicki.

SUBJECT: 1970 AND 1971 FORD
LOCATION: OUTDOOR
CAMERA/FILM: 8X10 VIEW CAMERA/EKTACHROME TRANSPARENCIES
ART DIRECTOR: JOHN DIGNAN

Ford or, more specifically, its agency, J. Walter Thompson, routinely commissioned experimental or exploratory photography for the purposes of designing and planning its advertising. As a rule, such pictures rarely found their way into actual ads, because the photography was done long before campaign ideas were in place and because we very often shot pre-production prototypes that weren't exactly "right." However, from this experimental shoot, one photo did survive and was featured in the introductory ad for the 1970 Torino.

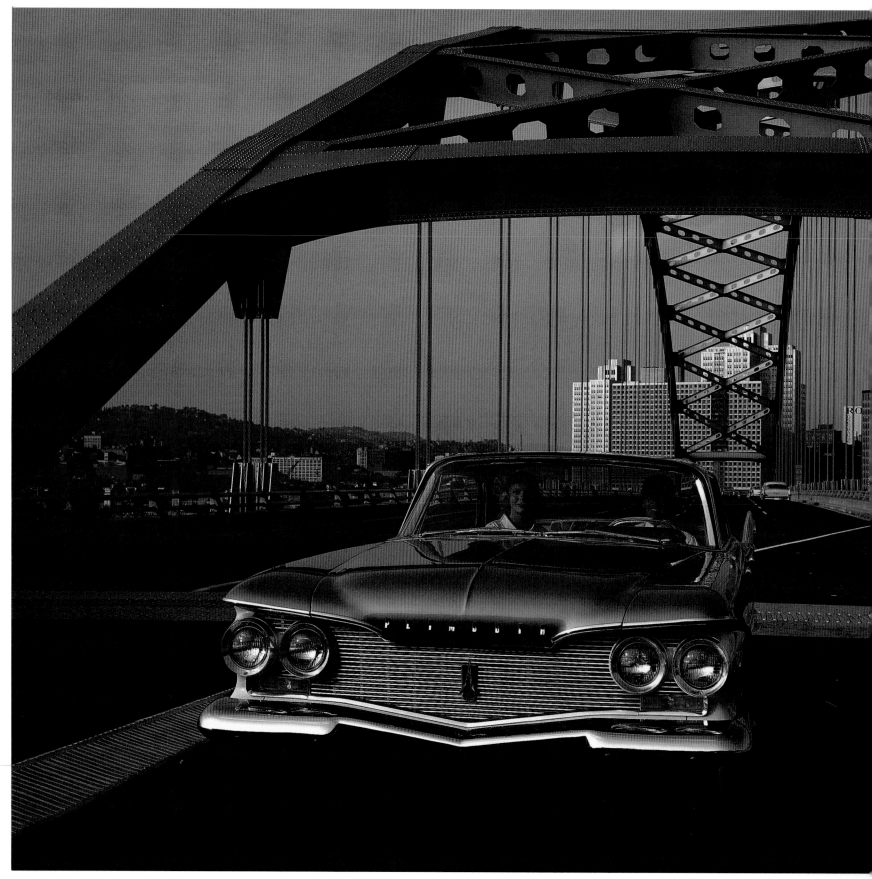

SUBJECT: PLYMOUTH
LOCATION: OUTDOOR
CAMERA/FILM: 8X10 VIEW CAMERA/EKTACHROME TRANSPARENCIES
ART DIRECTOR: BOB DUNNING

Although the car was always the star, it was a rare occasion when people weren't an important part of a picture. The fact is, you could be spot-on when it came to the sheet metal, but if the people weren't right, the shot was a bust. These pictures show two of the many fine models I had the pleasure to work with. Smiling out over the steering wheel of that 1960 Plymouth on a bridge in Pittsburgh is Bill Bixby. He became better known as Eddie's father and the Incredible Hulk. Alongside him is Beverly Penberthy. She played a part in a great many Boulevard pictures and also went on to become a noted actress. Of course, not all of the people who appeared in our pictures were always professionals. In the dockside scene, Beverly Penberthy is supported by a cast of characters that included the actual crew members of this ship and two of our clients. The center two customs officers were agency art directors Marty Lieberman and Bob Dunning.

SUBJECT: PLYMOUTH
LOCATION: VARIOUS OUTDOOR
CAMERA/FILM: 2-1/4 SINGLE LENS REFLEX/COLOR NEGATIVES
ART DIRECTOR: BOB DUNNING

To my knowledge, this was the first and perhaps the only time that an entire campaign was shot on 2-1/4-inch color negative film and reproduced from color prints. I decided to do so because Plymouth wanted a very large number of more or less candid pictures of cars and people in many different locations. Compared to positive transparencies, shooting with negative film can save a tremendous amount of time. This is because you can control exposure and color in the printing process. So every time you fire the camera you have a chance of getting a potentially usable picture, whereas when shooting transparencies we'd always make a whole series of "bracketed" exposures for every picture. The downside to working from negatives is that you must make a set of proofs to see what you have before you set about to make final prints. At the time, negative color film was a relatively new and unknown commodity, but it and the 2-1/4-inch cameras actually worked very well. The only real glitch came as one of the brochures was about to go to press. At the last minute, someone at the agency commented that a shot, which had been approved for the Valiant cover, showed Miss Penberthy in a pose that was a bit too candid. A furor ensued as we scrambled to find a tamer picture. Despite its speed and efficiency, color negative film would not go on to gain wide acceptance in the automobile advertising business.

SUBJECT: LINCOLN CONTINENTAL
LOCATION: OUTDOOR
CAMERA/FILM: 8X10 VIEW CAMERA/EKTACHROME TRANSPARENCY
ART DIRECTOR: WILLIAM MULLEN

Mickey handled Boulevard's business and finances, while I handled Boulevard's personnel and facilities. As a result, it was somewhat understandable that people were inclined to associate me with our studios and to think of me as "Mister Inside." At least this was the perception of the editor at Eastman Kodak Company's *Applied Photography* magazine when he decided to do a feature on Boulevard's outdoor photography. He had assumed that all of the pictures he'd selected were Mickey's and was mightily embarrassed when he initially attributed this picture to him. That we were associated with different specialties was good for business, but in fact we both shot everywhere and anywhere.

SUBJECT: PACKARD
LOCATION: NEW CENTER PHOTOGRAPHIC STUDIO
CAMERA/FILM: 8X10 VIEW CAMERA/EKTACHROME TRANSPARENCIES
ART DIRECTOR: MACK STANLEY

These pictures actually predate the founding of Boulevard Photographic. They were part of the first campaign that Mickey and I did for Mack Stanley who would become one of Boulevard's best clients.

Produced for the 1954 Packard sales brochures, these pictures represent one of the first major applications of tent lighting in car photography. And these were true tent pictures—meaning that the entire set was inside the lighting tent with only a small hole to allow the camera to peek through. Further complicating

things was the fact that, in those days, the speed of Ektachrome film was very slow. And although the lighting provided inside the tent was uniform, it was not very bright. As a result, exposure times were of astronomical duration—20, 30, or even 40 seconds—which meant models had to hold their poses a very long time. Nevertheless, in 1954, this was considered breakthrough stuff.

The backgrounds were designed by the fashion artist René Bouché, who actually came to the studio and made sketches that were then painted by Roy Jackson, who became a well-known Western artist. But at the time it was Bouché who was famous. During the shoot, Mickey asked Bouché to sign a little caricature he'd made of him. Bouché was flattered, but declined, saying, "The picture is free, but the signature is very expensive."

SUBJECT: 1968 OLDSMOBILES
LOCATION: BOULEVARD STUDIO CAMERA/FILM: 8X10 VIEW
CAMERA/EKTACHROME TRANSPARENCIES
ART DIRECTORS: MACK STANLEY AND PAUL WONSACK

This was the first in a series of three consecutive advertising campaigns I did with Mack Stanley years later when he was on the Oldsmobile account. I originally devised the concept for Chevrolet (top left). They bought it, but decided not to follow through after sitting on it for a couple of months. With nothing to lose, I took the samples over to Mack Stanley. He loved the idea and actually used my Chevrolet samples to sell Oldsmobile on the concept that combined youthful "lifestyle" images with pictures of cars.
The idea was pretty simple, but the work was very complex because it was all done on original film, double-exposing the background photographs into the photos of the cars. At first, getting the backgrounds and foregrounds to work together proved to be a nightmare. The backgrounds tended to overpower the foregrounds. Eventually, I found I could balance the two by making very soft, very flat, very muddy looking prints for the backgrounds, which when double-exposed with the foreground shots, picked up just enough contrast to remain clear but slightly muted behind the car.

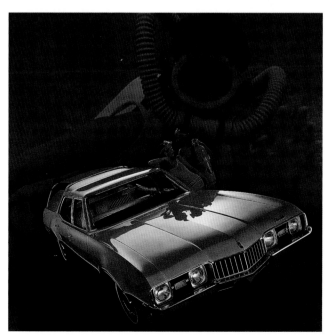

SUBJECT: 1969 OLDSMOBILES
LOCATION: BOULEVARD STUDIO
CAMERA/FILM: 8X10 VIEW CAMERA/EKTACHROME TRANSPARENCIES
ART DIRECTORS: MACK STANLEY AND PAUL WONSACK

For 1969, Oldsmobile was again targeting younger buyers. The theme was "Youngmobile thinking, now playing at Oldsmobile," which suggested a theatrical motif that blended the old and new. Mack Stanley wanted to continue using multiple images. However, based on the previous year's experience, we decided it would be easier to actually shoot the cars and models in front of huge backgrounds. Once again, what sounded like a simple idea turned out to be very complicated. This time, however, the problems were legal rather than technical. We had originally intended to use blowups of actual old-time movie stills for the backgrounds. But then, Oldsmobile's legal department got a look at one of the prototype ads. And although they liked what they saw, they wanted to see releases from all the people in the background photographs. The mere fact that most of the actors were dead didn't meant we wouldn't have to track down and pay for the rights to their visages. This posed a legal hassle that was deemed too complicated and expensive to undertake. Stanley, however, was undaunted. He gave me the go-ahead to recreate all of the original movie art using look-alike models and props. This proved to be a major undertaking that was also an awful lot of fun. Ultimately, the whole thing came together beautifully, and most people never questioned whether the background pictures were real. For 1970, I teamed up with Stanley and his associate Paul Wonsack to do another "lifestyle" campaign. Shortly thereafter, Mack Stanley, a long-time supporter and friend, passed away.

Olds Delta 88 Royale: The bold and the beautiful.

Meet our new top-of-the-line 88. It brings youthful flair and excitement to the big-car world.
  Sporty touches everywhere: Vinyl top. Pinstriping. Chrome fender louvers. Custom sport seat. All yours. All standard.
  These are only openers. Delta 88 Royale has a lot more going for it. Rocket 455 V-8. Roomier, easier-to-load trunk. Road-leveling 124-inch wheel-base. The many thoughtful new GM safety features.
  Royale—youngmobile thinking in a big, beautiful package —at your Olds dealer's now. **Escape from the ordinary.**

MICKEY McGUIRE
Artist and Magician

"Just to make a picture of what exists in nature isn't always correct, but if any contrivance you use is obvious to any intelligent viewer, you have failed."
—Mickey McGuire

SUBJECT: MITSUBISHI
LOCATION: OUTDOOR
CAMERA/FILM: 8X10 VIEW CAMERA/EKTACHROME TRANSPARENCY
ART DIRECTOR: DARRYL LOMAS

It was my job to shoot *all* of the pictures for the Mitsubishi catalog for 1986. The client, however, was planning to pick up a picture of a racing car from someone else. I convinced the art director that I could shoot the *entire* catalog, and I got him to get me a Mitsubishi race car to shoot. I made this picture in a parking lot. This is a double-motion-rig picture, in which the car and the background were both moving, but in opposite directions. The motion rig was used to pull the car. In the foreground, some lines were swept onto the pavement. To create the background, the side of a truck was covered with black cloth, and we put some strips of colored paper on it to accentuate the illusion of motion. When I shot the picture, the motion rig was pulling the car in one direction, and the truck moved in the opposite direction. It effectively doubled the illusion of speed. The art director was delighted, and so was I because I could say I shot *all* the pictures in the catalog.

SUBJECT: FORD THUNDERBIRD
LOCATION: OUTDOOR
CAMERA/FILM: 2-1/4 SINGLE LENS REFLEX/TRANSPARENCIES
ART DIRECTOR: VAN STITH

We were on an ad shoot for Thunderbird in Florida, and the advertising theme that year was "The Private World of Thunderbird." We shot in many lonely places, and I thought as long as we were down there around the islands, I would look for an island to put the car on—that's a very private world. We looked at a number of islands but I couldn't find one that was small enough to show that it was an island without making the car look dinky—clients hate that. So, I decided to make my own little island.
We started with a rented barge. I had outriggers built on the sides, which were covered with plywood, burlap, and sand to create a sloping beach. Then we hired a greens man to bring in some palm trees, hedges and other flora. We got a tugboat and tugged our creation out through the Miami River into Key Biscayne, in front of a Catholic girls' school. We shot at dusk and left our island in the river overnight so we could shoot again at dawn. The next morning, when school was starting, all the girls came running down to the shore, arguing with each other, "That island was there." "No, it's never been there." "Well, maybe it was, but how did they get the car on it?" They all fell silent when the tugboat came and towed our island away.

SUBJECT: JAGUAR
LOCATION: OUTDOOR
CAMERA/FILM: 8X10 VIEW CAMERA/EKTACHROME TRANSPARENCY
ART DIRECTOR: MICKEY McGUIRE

This was set up as an example of how we shot automobiles for filming an Eastman Kodak *Visions and View* videotape. Each year they would feature a different studio, and this time they chose Boulevard. Jimmy did a motion rig in the studio, and I did a car picture on location. They filmed me making this picture of the Jaguar. The point was to demonstrate how to control the color and use controls to make the picture: filtration, polarizing screen, drop cloths, white cards in front, a little light on the girl's face, etc.

SUBJECT: FORD
LOCATION: OUTDOOR
CAMERA/FILM: 8X10 VIEW CAMERA/EKTACHROME TRANSPARENCY
ART DIRECTOR: MICKEY McGUIRE

I was photographing the 1965 Ford annual report, making all kinds of illustrations of various products that would be interspersed throughout the book. I had to make a picture of a couple of cars, so, being in the middle of my chess mania in those days, I thought, why not try to do a picture of two people playing chess on a very large scale. So, we made a big chess board, got the big chess pieces, and set up the two cars with two people playing a game of chess. I wasn't sure if Ford would like it, but it seemed like a wild and wonderful thing to do. Ford thought so, too, and they were happy to use it in their annual report.

SUBJECT: FORD
LOCATION: BOULEVARD STUDIO
CAMERA/FILM: 8X10 VIEW CAMERA/EKTACHROME TRANSPARENCY
ART DIRECTOR: JACK FISCHER

The fireworks in this picture were taken from slides that my assistant, Walter Sternicki, had—he loved to go shoot fireworks displays. I took his slides, put them in the front projection machine, and set up everything in the studio. To tie everything together, I gave the girl a sparkler. This is an example of using front projection in the studio, and it was one of a series that contains some of my favorite pictures.

SUBJECT: CHEVROLET CORSICA
LOCATION: OUTDOOR
CAMERA/FILM: 2 1/4 SINGLE LENS REFLEX/TRANSPARENCIES
ART DIRECTOR: BOB FORLENZA

The interesting thing about this picture is that the ad agency was dead
against shooting on 8x10 cameras and doing what they called, "phony
stuff." They insisted on real motion shots. But I convinced an art director
that I could make a shot using our rig that they wouldn't know wasn't a real
motion shot. And I could do it under absolutely controlled circumstances. So
I set this one up. It's a double-motion-rig picture with a truck in the
background. The location was a cemetery parking lot near our studio, and I
shot it with a 2-1/4-inch camera. The deal I made with the art director was
that I wouldn't charge for the rig if he didn't tell the client I used it.
Everybody loved the result. But other than the art director and me, no one
knew it wasn't a real motion shot.

SUBJECT: FORD MAVERICK
LOCATION: OUTDOOR
CAMERA/FILM: 8X10 VIEW CAMERA/EKTACHROME TRANSPARENCY
ART DIRECTOR: VAN STITH

This is the product of an experimental shoot. The idea was to show a Maverick in an Old West setting. I got a bunch of old western pictures and dressed the models in western garb, then posed them together. I shot the picture at dusk and used neutral-density gels to control and accentuate the lighting. I don't believe it was ever used in an ad, but it was a lot of fun getting all those pictures and putting the models in western outfits.

SUBJECT: FORD TORINO WAGON
LOCATION: OUTDOOR
CAMERA/FILM: 8X10 VIEW CAMERA/EKTACHROME TRANSPARENCY
ART DIRECTOR: JACK FISCHER

Experimental shoots were a good part of my business with Ford's J. Walter Thompson agency. We were constantly wracking our brains to come up with new ideas of things to do. In this case, I said, "What the hell. Let's take a station wagon out to the valley." We went out to where Westlake Village now stands, a huge suburb northwest of Los Angeles. Then, it was a beautiful, arid mountain range with hills that looked just like Africa to me. So I got a bunch of stuffed animals and went out and made this picture. Again, I don't think this ever became an ad, but it was the kind of picture that sure kept them hiring me.

SUBJECT: 1968 FORD
LOCATION: OUTDOOR
CAMERA/FILM: 8X10 VIEW CAMERA/EKTACHROME
TRANSPARENCIES
ART DIRECTOR: VAN STITH

On an experimental shoot down in Florida, I came up
with a concept that I illustrated a number of different
ways. I called it "A day in the life of a Ford owner." The
idea was to show new Fords along with people at work
and at play. To do that, I took a group of models and
shot them having fun and doing the sorts of things that
people do during the day—enjoying themselves on the
beach, zooming around in a speedboat, going to work,
playing tennis, or just goofing off. I shot these pictures
on 2-1/4-inch black-and-white film and then made
prints that I then used in the color portraits of the cars
shot at dusk.

The problem with experimental photographs such as
these was that we would make them in January and
February, but the cars wouldn't be announced until
September. We'd make lots of pictures that were used
by the clients to pick angles and locations, but by the
time they were ready to make the real advertising,
they'd had lots of meetings and were tired of looking at
the same pictures. So, all these experimental pictures
would be put away, and we would go out and shoot the
"real" stuff. By this time their thinking was all
tightened, and nine times out of ten the "real" pictures
weren't nearly as adventurous or interesting as the
ones we'd make on experimental shoots.

SUBJECT: LINCOLN
LOCATION: OUTDOOR
CAMERA/FILM: 8X10 VIEW CAMERA/EKTACHROME TRANSPARENCY
ART DIRECTOR: ROCCO CAMPANELLI

This picture may look simple, but it involved a lot of planning. I'd scouted this Malibu Beach location with an eye toward figuring out where the sun would be. What I wanted was the sun's light, but not the sun itself, in the picture. In this shot, the sun is just out of frame in the upper right-hand corner. Of course the trick was to get everything set up and ready to go at the moment when the sun would be in the right position. In addition to calculating exposures, figuring out the filters, and composing the picture, getting those big Lincolns out onto a soft, sandy beach was no easy task. It took four or five hours to set up the shot, with a lot of that time spent grooming the sand to make it look as though the Lincolns had landed there by magic.

SUBJECT: CHRYSLER
LOCATION: OUTDOOR
CAMERA/FILM: 8X10 VIEW CAMERA/EKTACHROME TRANSPARENCY
ART DIRECTOR: MICKEY McGUIRE

This was an early sample picture I made to show how we could create a rainy night. The shot was taken in Royal Oak, Michigan, across the street from the fire station. Because my old scout master was the fire chief, he was happy to turn on the hoses to provide the "rain" and wet down the scene—and the photographer. I used my own car, and the scene was lit using old-style flashbulbs.

SUBJECT: 1969 FORD MUSTANG
LOCATION: OUTDOOR
CAMERA/FILM: 8X10 VIEW CAMERA/EKTACHROME TRANSPARENCY
ART DIRECTOR: VAN STITH

This is a shot in what I call my "interruptive" series. The idea was to catch people in the act of doing something natural. I wanted it to look as though a photographer had just happened on the scene and said, "Hey, you!" And when the person turned around, someone snapped the picture. Of course, the shots were all carefully staged in order to make the car appear its very best.

SUBJECT: 1975 DODGE COLT
LOCATION: OUTDOOR
CAMERA/FILM: 8X10 VIEW CAMERA/EKTACHROME TRANSPARENCY
ART DIRECTOR: MIKE LABIAK

Daytona Beach is one of the few beaches you can drive on, so it was a popular place to photograph cars. One of the things that made it so attractive is that when the tide comes in and laps up underneath the car, it makes a beautiful setting. The only problem is you really have to hurry to get a shot. If you wait too long, wave after wave rolls in under the car and the car begins to sink. And if you're not paying attention, you may not notice that the car has sunk in deep enough that you can't drive it away. I didn't lose the car here, but I did get a beautiful picture.

SUBJECT: FORD PROBE
LOCATION: STUDIO
CAMERA/FILM: 8X10 VIEW CAMERA/EKTACHROME TRANSPARENCY
ART DIRECTOR: ANDY NELSON

This is an example of a "teaser" picture. There are times when a car maker has a new product that they're not ready to show to the public, but they want to "tease" their interest. This was a prototype of the Ford Probe that I shot in a large Ford garage in Palm Springs. The motion is phony—I used striated grease in front of the lens to blur the taillights and the highlights on the wheels. The bright highlights on the wheels were made with small spot lights. The meteor shooting through the background was added as a double exposure.

SUBJECT: TOYOTA CELICA
LOCATION: STUDIO
CAMERA/FILM: 8X10 VIEW CAMERA/EKTACHROME TRANSPARENCIES
ART DIRECTOR: NIPPON DESIGN CENTER

We often found ourselves shooting prototypes that were under tight wraps. In this case, Toyota had a new Celica that they wouldn't allow out of the studio, much less out of the country. So I went to Japan to shoot it. They wanted a variety of pictures. To create a beauty shot, I decided to make an elegant dockside setting. I wanted to use a brick floor so I laid out a little pattern as an example of how it should look, then went to lunch. With typical Japanese efficiency, the whole thing was completed by the time we got back. The floor was laid, the little flower boxes were in place. All I had to do was set up the lighting and photograph the car. The boat in the background came from a picture I'd found in a magazine, put up on a board, and double exposed into the car pictures to make it look like it was outside.

I also made a performance shot of the Celica in the studio. This is an example of phony motion using a combination of dust on the floor and grease in front of the lens. An interesting thing about this shot is the reflection in the hood. What appeared to be real buildings were actually cardboard cutouts that were hand-painted in the studio.

SUBJECT: CHEVROLET CAMARO
LOCATION: OUTDOOR
CAMERA/FILM: 8X10 VIEW CAMERA/EKTACHROME TRANSPARENCY
ART DIRECTOR: BOB FORLENZA

This is one of my favorite pictures because it illustrates an oft-told story—a cop hiding behind a billboard waiting for his prey. Hard as we tried, we could never find the right road with a billboard in just the right place. So we found a desolate, desert road in Southern California and constructed our own billboard out of old, weathered wood to make it look like it had been there forever.

SUBJECT: LINCOLN
LOCATION: OUTDOOR
CAMERA/FILM: 8X10 VIEW CAMERA/EKTACHROME TRANSPARENCY
ART DIRECTOR: ROCCO CAMPANELLI

The model in this shot for a Lincoln ad just happens to be Tom Selleck who was a great model and a great guy to work with. To say he was cooperative would be an understatement. He would help polish the cars and help set up the shot, then he'd run in, strike a pose, and always look great.

SUBJECT: LINCOLN
LOCATION: OUTDOOR
CAMERA/FILM: 8X10 VIEW CAMERA/EKTACHROME TRANSPARENCY
ART DIRECTOR: JONAS GOLD

The art director wanted to show moody people in moody settings. For this Lincoln ad, he envisioned a smug, middle-aged, bald guy with a bad attitude. The guy we got was actually a very nice insurance salesman. So in order to get him in the mood, I kept telling him, "Just turn around and say f— you!" It appeared to be just the right motivation.

SUBJECT: JAGUAR
LOCATION: STUDIO
CAMERA/FILM: 8X10 VIEW CAMERA/EKTACHROME TRANSPARENCY
ART DIRECTOR: MICKEY McGUIRE

The best thing about the motion rig was that it could give art directors control over what goes into a picture. When you're sailing down a highway in the back of a station wagon, with the art director in the front seat shouting back, "Did you get it?" And you're saying, "Yeah, I think so," the art director doesn't have much confidence. All he was doing was going along for the ride. But the motion rig gave art directors a chance to really get in there and direct. To demonstrate what the rig could do, I invited a number of clients into the studio. And to make sure they remembered the experience, each one got a photograph of himself or herself "in motion" in this classic XKE.

SUBJECT: JAGUAR XJS
LOCATION: OUTDOOR
CAMERA/FILM: 8X10 VIEW CAMERA/EKTACHROME TRANSPARENCY
ART DIRECTOR: MARCE MAYHEW

This is one of my favorite pictures of one of my favorite cars. It's an example of everything working out perfectly. I started with a bright, sunset sky, and as I began to tone it down using my usual controls, a beautiful scene began to emerge with the color and highlights of the car harmonizing perfectly with the sky.

SUBJECT: CHRYSLER 300
LOCATION: OUTDOOR
CAMERA/FILM: 8X10 VIEW CAMERA/EKTACHROME TRANSPARENCY
ART DIRECTOR: MICKEY McGUIRE

This picture was actually shot on a golf course in the bright, mid-day sun. I was on a Chrysler shoot, and while hanging around waiting for sunset, I said, "Why don't we go out—I've got something I'd like to try." I took this picture using flashbulbs. The trick was that I used indoor-type bulbs and indoor film, but took the shot outside. The clear flashbulbs gave a normal kind of light, while the ambient daylight was somewhat cool. By underexposing the background and using the flash, it gave the appearance of dusk even though it was high noon.

SUBJECT: LINCOLN
LOCATION: EASTERN MICHIGAN UNIVERSITY FIELD HOUSE
CAMERA/FILM: 8X10 VIEW CAMERA/EKTACHROME
TRANSPARENCIES
ART DIRECTOR: JIM ELLIOT

This was a big idea that required a big set and a big effort. The easy part was making the cars appear big. For that, we used our stretch film holders. But, the art director had also come up with the idea for some very large, very elaborate sets, and although it might have been possible to use scale models and double exposure, he insisted on doing everything life size. He wanted to construct giant sets, use real models and real trees. The only place we found that was big enough to accommodate the art director's vision was the Eastern Michigan University Field House. Clearly, it was big enough, but it wasn't without its problems. There were huge windows in the building, so in order to get steady light, we had to work at night. Unfortunately, the electrical system didn't have enough juice to power our lights, so we had to bring in generating trucks that ran through the night.

There were several different sets, and each took a week to construct. So this shoot went on for a very long time. Getting the trees in was also lots of fun. We had to get special permits to have the traffic lights removed along the route to the field house. And when we got the trees inside, the art director wanted them all sprayed white. It was a fussy job, because frankly, the art director was a very fussy kind of guy. But it made for some fantastic pictures.

SUBJECT: WALT DISNEY
LOCATION: DISNEYLAND
CAMERA/FILM: 8X10 VIEW CAMERA/EKTACHROME TRANSPARENCY
ART DIRECTOR: ANDY NELSON

This obviously isn't a car picture, but it was a result of some extra work I did while on an experimental shoot for Ford. J. Walter Thompson, which was Ford's advertising agency, also had the RCA Victor account. The people on the RCA business had come up with a theme line, "Color so real you think you're there," and asked for my help in finding a way to illustrate it. I ended up taking all of the guts out of a television set and used it to frame scenes which I set up at various locations. The client loved the results and, since it was my idea, I got the actual shooting assignment. And the first ad they wanted shot was to be in Disneyland with Walt Disney himself. I'd grown up with Walt Disney as one of my heroes. So when I was asked to take a picture of him, I was probably the most nervous photographer in the world. I shot him with his many colorful Disney characters. It was quite an experience to set it up and to control the background to emphasize what was going on behind the TV screen. I gelled everything but the picture tube area and used some grease to make the background a little bit softer. Mr. Disney turned out to be a patient and understanding model. I was a young man in my midtwenties and little did I know I'd be making history. This was one of the last pictures made of Walt Disney who died shortly after the ad first ran. Disney characters © Disney Enterprises, Inc./ Used by permission from Disney Enterprises, Inc.

"This picture grew out of a whim," confesses Mickey McGuire, partner in Detroit's Boulevard Photographic, Inc., and for the last 18 years one of the world's top automotive photographers. "If it has wheels," he says, "I shoot it. "I wanted to do a kind of Mondrian black-and-white color transparency of a car," he remembers. "I didn't really did a lot of pictures. Along the way, I decided to go with a black girl and a white girl, a black outfit and a white outfit, and reflections of black and white on a black car."
The checkerboard pattern on the 1972 Chrysler was produced by rigging black and white overhead reflectors in the studio. After that, it took McGuire 1½ days of effect he was after. He got it with an 8 x 10-inch view camera, a 9½-inch lens, and EKTACHROME Film 6116, Type B. The light was 3200 K bounced off the reflectors above and to the sides of the set.

IMAGINATION DOES IT—
with Kodak products.

159

INDEX

10. CAMBRIDGE MODERN

Despite the weather, New England is one of the easiest places to restore an old home. Our housing styles are well defined, with abundant examples—both good and bad—of authentic Victorians, Capes, and Colonials. New Englanders have an affinity for these styles, and our tradesmen have the skills to work them.

It's as if New England has its own housing vernacular— and everybody is fluent. So you wouldn't think Cambridge, Massachusetts, with some of the richest housing stock in the country, would be the location of one of our most challenging restorations. But it was.

BEFORE

LEFT: The homeowner met with five architects and had three scale models fully constructed before he settled on this design, shown in the fourth model.

FACING PAGE: The original home was designed by a student of Walter Gropius, father of the Bauhaus style. The rear of the house has a wall of glass overlooking the home's most appealing feature: its backyard.

When we came across the Cambridge house, it was decidedly more modern than any home we had worked on to date, and this excited a bunch of "old house" guys. The home had been built in 1950, during a period that gave us the Bauhaus and International styles, with both their fondness for function over form and their aversion to ornamentation. Accordingly, our house was stripped of detail. The building wasn't much more than a series of red boxes, angular on most sides, with a roof that pitched inward to its center like butterfly wings. The house sat low in a bowl-shaped yard and was rotting slowly from the pond that persistently formed around it every spring. Thick bushes and trees surrounded the house and made it nearly indistinguishable from the street. Only its dark and cavernous carport—a terrible vestige of the 1950s—could be seen clearly as it lurched toward the road.

The house's style was loosely based on the Bauhaus school, founded by Walter Gropius in post–World War I Germany. Gropius eventually landed just a few blocks from this house, at Harvard University, after fleeing Nazi Germany and taking the dean's post at the Harvard School of Architecture (today the Harvard University Graduate School of Design). I have a hunch that, had Gropius strolled by the

house as we came upon it fifty-six years after its construction, he would be pleased only with the intent, not the lasting result.

The current homeowner, George Mabry, was a longtime fan of our television show and a self-proclaimed lover of fine homes. These are the sorts of people we meet all the time; in fact, we seek them out. But in this case, George's pronounced love of fine homes seemed . . . well, odd, given his house's state of disrepair. What sort of love affair was he having with the red vertical siding wrapping his home and rotting on two sides? George quickly assured us that it wasn't the house he was in love with—it was the location, an indisputably attractive lot less than two miles from Harvard Square. And he was in love with the idea of renovating his home.

Usually, when a homeowner tells us he's been thinking about a renovation for ten years, we proceed with caution. When he goes on to tell us he's worked with five architects during that period, we head for the door. But in this case, we headed to the basement instead—to look at four fully constructed architectural models that represented four completely different plans for a renovation of George's tired but not-so-old modern house. The wildly different styles of the models made it clear that

FACING PAGE: The house was mostly hidden behind trees and bushes, leaving the carport as the property's defining feature, something about which neither the homeowner nor his neighbors were thrilled.

FACING PAGE INSET: Flat roofs are rarely flat. This house had a leaky butterfly roof that pitched to the center.

TOP LEFT: We stripped much of the original house away and expanded it just slightly to accommodate a small addition. The newly poured concrete, seen here on the side and front of the house, was all we added.

TOP RIGHT: With the addition of stucco and a new stone-clad central fireplace, the house started to take on a new look; less Bauhaus and more Prairie-style.

AFTER

George was perplexed. We were intrigued. We had never worked on such a young and modern house, and its pedigree—designed by a student of Gropius himself—interested us. But it was George's predicament—what to do—that was the real allure. His dilemma became our dilemma.

So what do you do with a fifty-five-year-old house loosely interpreting the Bauhaus style, modern and possibly provocative in its day but definitely no longer so? Do you adhere strictly to the original style—even if you're not a fan? Do you start fresh and take advantage of a beautiful lot and cues from the proud examples of more traditional New England architecture all around you? Or do you split the difference and create something reminiscent of the original but more to your liking?

Our team decided to split the difference and quickly took up the renovation. Concentrating first on the exterior, we knocked down the carport and stripped the house of its three-inch-wide vertical red siding that was rotting on both ends. The siding was a monolithic wrap devoid of detail, and with it gone, we were able to install a variety of new materials to great effect.

Stucco became the primary new surface but not the most interesting. We completely wrapped a front corner of the house in reclaimed redwood that had been

FACING PAGE: The new chimney takes center stage and the rest of the house was designed to "pinwheel" away from it. Each rectilinear form stops at the chimney, never breaking through its strong vertical line.

ABOVE LEFT AND RIGHT: The waterfall appears to spring magically from the stone wall, and the bluestone steps are set on a hidden stringer, giving the illusion that they support themselves. The water flows the length of the house before starting the trip all over again.

RIGHT: Most of the house is clad in stucco, but on this important corner we used redwood reclaimed from huge olive oil barrels. It still had a slight shimmer and gave off an olive scent when it was cut.

FACING PAGE: We kept the glass across the back of the house and added more. A two-story staircase has a glass wall looking out over the apple tree; a guest bedroom has a wall of glass, too, as does the new third-floor study, which the homeowner likens to working in a tree house.

used to make huge olive-oil barrels. The character of this wood, silky and almost glistening, was a joy to look at, and any skeptic of its prominent use was won over when oil-infused scraps of the wood were tossed into the fireplace and perfumed the otherwise cold and dusty job site.

We repaired an old chimney and added a new one. The new chimney grew out of the foundation and climbed one and a half stories above the new third floor. It was long and narrow and it became the new dominant shape of the house, a rectilinear form that was repeated again with clerestory windows, tall sidelights, new half-story façades, and the vertical redwood siding, as pleasant to look at as it was to smell.

We wrapped the chimney in a second material—stone veneer—that was also used on two low-slung walls in the new front yard. The stone chimney protruded beyond all other façades but slipped back into the house as well, framing part of the new entryway

BELOW LEFT: The chimney appears in and out of the house at the same time thanks to a tall window that runs up the chimney's length and is set into the stones, no more than inch. The clerestory window above makes this a preferred place to sit.

BELOW RIGHT: The bent-brass staircase balusters overlap to create a pleasing and unique form. This landing looks out onto the apple tree in the backyard.

and continuing into the house as part of a one-and-a-half-story fireplace off the new dining room. Wood, glass, stucco, and stone became the new face of the house and transformed it from a stark, monolithic box into a warm and varied collection of rooms and shapes that seemed to pinwheel out from the now prominent chimney.

The interior design called for very little trim; just a narrow, quarter-inch-wide channel around the windows and doors, making for austere, almost sharp corners. The design also called for the new oak doors to be stained black and for a new staircase, made with exposed steel stringers and cold brass balusters, to be built, aggressively dominating the house's entryway. The combination of all these chilly materials had me thinking "unlivable." It also had me wondering if I'd ever warm up to the modern style.

Before our Cambridge project, I wasn't a big fan of modern homes. I found some designs interesting and appreciated the fact that their free form allowed for open spaces and expansive views not often found in more traditional houses. But I never found the modern style very livable, and as work progressed on the interior of George's house—with all those cold materials—my skepticism persisted.

ABOVE: This is one of the largest rooms in the house but is broken into three distinct spaces: two seating areas and a dining room. Different ceiling heights, lighting, and control of the interior and exterior views make it feel like separate rooms.

RIGHT: The staircase greets visitors as soon as they walk through the door and is a collection of materials: five-inch-thick teak treads, steel stringers, brass baluster, and a stone veneer along the back wall.

FACING PAGE TOP LEFT: The homeowner is an audiophile and has an impressive collection of vinyl records, which he proudly displays in this alcove off the living room.

FACING PAGE BOTTOM LEFT: Even though this alcove is part of the dining room, it becomes a separate space with the chair flanked by millwork and turned toward the window. Even with the window shade down, sunlight fills this intimate corner.

FACING PAGE BOTTOM RIGHT: Once the homeowner saw the richness of the reclaimed redwood we used on the exterior of the house, he decided to use more of it on the living room wall around the fireplace.

In the end, however, what George designed became one of the warmest, most livable houses I ever worked on with *This Old House*, and I had a complete change of heart when it comes to modern homes. The materials—steel, stone, glass—were paired with soft cherry cabinets, more reclaimed redwood inside, floor-to-ceiling cabinetry to house an earthy pottery collection, and even a tasteful acoustic wall made of fabric that occupied a prominent place in our audiophile's living room. The steel-and-brass staircase was topped with five-inch-thick teak treads and wooden handrails that were soft underfoot and under hand. Even the black-stained doors seemed warm and welcoming.

In the end, George was triumphant. His patience paid off, and even though he wasn't slavishly faithful to the Bauhaus style, he did create a modern home that I suspect would have pleased the old masters. If our friend Walter Gropius were to walk the streets of Cambridge again and pass by George's house, he might not say, "Ah, a Bauhaus"—but I'm sure we'd hear him say "Ah, a *fine* house."

LEFT: The homeowner enjoys entertaining so there is a full-service wet bar off the living room. Most of our crew took advantage of this feature—more than once.

PAGE 212: The designer called for dark tiles in the master bathroom that were similar in tone to the dark trim throughout the house. I was skeptical of all the dark trim until I saw it on the walls; it was a perfect choice.

PAGE 213 LEFT: A leak in the kitchen sky-light during construction ruined the kitchen millwork—twice! But it became the perfect opportunity to upgrade the entire room with new cherry cabinets.

PAGE 213 UPPER RIGHT: A flat-panel design on the front of the island matches the style of the cabinet doors.

PAGE 213 LOWER RIGHT: The living room flows easily into the kitchen. A small, round table between the two spaces is flanked by a built-in console, also made of warm cherry.

FACING PAGE: We used different materials and ceiling heights to temper the wide-open floor plan of the living room and kitchen. Notice how slate adjoins wood on the floor and how the ceiling is high near the wall of glass but drops down in the living room and at the kitchen soffits.

ABOVE: Two stone walls protect the house from the busy street, and the water feature drowns out city noises. It's as if the modern house is fortified against its surroundings and set apart from the otherwise traditional neighborhood. A classic Victorian home is barely visible over the walls and through the trees.

Close Up
Norm Abram

Norm has a favorite spot in his house—the house he built himself. It's a large vaulted room that contains the kitchen, dining, and family rooms. The rest of the house is stick built but this room is a grand timber frame with large posts and beams made from Sitka spruce and Port Orford Cedar. Some years ago Norm wrote about that space: "I take so much pleasure in studying the frame. I look at its sturdiness and know it will be standing for many decades, maybe a century or two. In our part of the country, that's what one wants in a home: a sense of durability."

And he's right. We want our homes to be durable; we want them to last. And not just our homes, we want lots of things to last: our tools, our friendships, our legacies, the love we share with our families. It's a powerful sentiment, this idea that things and people will always be there.

And it's a fitting observation from a guy who's pretty durable himself. Think about this: Norm's been on *This Old House* for thirty-two years now. He just wrapped up twenty-one years of making *The New Yankee Workshop*. In any profession, that's a long time. In television, it's the very definition of durable.

People stop me all the time to say hello or shake hands, and invariably they end up asking about Norm. "How is he?" they ask, or "Tell him I said hi." They say it as if they know him; as if Norm knows them! That's what happens when things last. We become attached to them, we rely on them. And after thirty-two years, we rely on and are attached to Norm as much as ever.

Index

Resource Guide

Riverside Colonial Revival
Location: Auburndale, MA
Year: 2010
General Contractor: Silva Brothers Construction
Architect: H. Christina Chu Architect
Interior Design: Melissa Gulley Interior Design
Landscape Design: Nawada Landscape Design, Inc.

New England Farmhouse
Location: Carlisle, MA
Year: 2004
General Contractor: Silva Brothers Construction
Architect: Jeremiah Eck, AIA
Interior Design: Bovey Steers Design Group, Charles Spada Interiors, Eric Cohler Design Incorporated, Frank Roop Design Interiors, Lisa Newman Interiors, LLC, Mally Skok Design, Mark Hampton, Inc., Marshall Whitman Design
Landscape Design: SiteCreative Landscape Architecture

Second Empire Victorian
Location: Roxbury, MA
Year: 2009
General Contractor: Wellington Design & Construction Company
Architect: Michael Washington Architects
Interior Design: Patricia McDonagh Interior Design
Landscape Design: The Designery, YouthBuild Boston

Brooklyn Brownstone
Location: Brooklyn, NY
Year: 2008
General Contractor: M.R.S. Inc.
Architect: Susanne Lyn, RA
Interior Design: Carole Freehauf Design
Landscape Design: Chelsea Garden Center

Weston Timber Frame
Location: Weston, MA
Year: 2008
General Contractor: Silva Brothers Construction, Bensonwod
Architect: Design-build by Bensonwood
Landscape Design: Thomas Wirth Associates Inc.

Dutch Colonial Revival
Location: Newton, MA
Year: 2009
General Contractor: Silva Brothers Construction
Architect: HP Rovinelli Architects
Landscape Design: K & R Tree and Landscape Co.

Shingle-Style Victorian
Location: Newton, MA
Year: 2007
General Contractor: Silva Brothers Construction
Architect: LDa Architects LLP
Interior Design: AbbeyK, Inc.
Landscape Design: SiteCreative Landscape Architecture

Texas Bungalow
Location: Austin, TX
Year: 2007
General Contractor: WM. T. Moore Construction, Inc.
Architect: Webber/Hanzlik Architects
Interior Design: Wildflower Organics
Landscape Design: Sunflower Design, Inc.

Spanish Revival
Location: Los Angeles, CA
Year: 2010
General Contractor: Home Front Design + Build
Architect: Design-build by Home Front Design + Build
Interior Design: Rachel Horn Interiors
Landscape Design: Melanie Williams Landscapes

Cambridge Modern
Location: Cambridge, MA
Year: 2005
General Contractor: Silva Brothers Construction
Architect: Ruhl Walker Architects
Interior Design: Todd Tsiang
Landscape Design: Gregory Lombardi Design, Inc.

For most projects:
Landscape contracting provided by Roger Cook, K&R Tree and Landscape Co.
Heating and cooling design consultation provided by Richard Trethewey, RST, Inc.

For a complete list of resources for each project, please visit www.ThisOldHouse.com.

Acknowledgments

Thanks to all of the people who had a hand in renovating and building these houses, from the homeowners to the television production team to the tradespeople who made the homes beautiful. Without their efforts and talents, there would be no book. Thanks to photographer Michael Casey, a true partner in this endeavor and a close friend. Mike worked with a terrific crew and does a good job recognizing them below. Thanks to Julie Mehegan, another close friend, for her early editing skills and her patience with the passive voice. Thanks to my colleagues at *This Old House* for their collaboration and advice. And finally, thanks to Eric Lupfer, Leslie Stoker, Dervla Kelly, LeAnna Weller Smith, Ivy McFadden, and the entire team at Stewart, Tabori & Chang.

Kevin O'Connor

I want to first thank my mom, Maryjane, who encouraged me to pursue my creative talent and do more with it, and my dad, Bill, who died eight years ago; though he never got to see me as a professional photographer, his memory pushes me to be the best I can be.

A big "thank ye" to my siblings, Kiz, Joe, and Cal. You are great friends and important role models, and I couldn't be where I am without you. To my in-laws, Kristin, Dez, Eileen and Derek, Neil and Cris, and Lynsey and Brian for your friendship and love. Thanks to Anne and Kent, Carole and KC, and Big Doug and Marcia for your pride in me as a photographer, father, and husband. And thanks to the extended Casey, Hughes, and Heffernan circle for always cheering me on and being there for me.

To Adam Krauth, who was huge throughout, whether on-set, as the keeper of all images, or during the neverending post-production stage. And a big thanks to our outstanding assistants: Todd Dionne, Dan Klempa, Adam Clear, Chris Rioux, Charles Lee, and Ryan Goodrich.

A very special thanks to two wonderful mentors, Estrellita Karsh and Bill Brett, who provided the finest professional guidance and endless encouragement.

A big thank-you to an important group of friends for their sound advice, support, and expertise: Jack Connors, Mike Sheehan, Karen Kaplan, Jim Ricciardi, Doug Arnold, Maureen Devaney, Ming Tsai, and the closer, Jeff Tully.

And lastly, to my great friend, O'C. Thanks so much for asking me to be a part of this.

Mike Casey